`*The Forensic Certified Public Accountant and the Christmas Donor's Trust Fund -*

Book Number Fou

By Dwight David Thrash CPA

MW00947930

AUTHOR'S NOTE

The characters are fictional, even though they appear to be real. This book is based on real accounting and forensic accounting. The author is a real Certified Public Accountant, Forensic Certified Public Accountant, and a Chartered Global Management Accountant in good standing.

For my parents, Dwight A. and Wanda, & my sister, Delesa and her family,

Thank you, for your support.

I love you.

Contents

Chapter 1 the Christmas Donor's Trust Fund

Let us begin by saying that a nice person called perhaps Santa Claus was left money from an infinite balance trust fund. This trust fund is infinite because no matter how much money is spent the account does not go down, even one cent. There is only one condition. That condition is that every cent that is spent must be used for the purpose of doing nice things for anyone that needs help. Of course, "It would be nice if you would give me all of your items." or "It would be nice if I can live rent-free in this apartment." or anything that would constitute "greed" would not be good for this "Santa Claus Trust Fund Account."

Santa Claus has to be very careful in whom Santa Claus trusts because the magic of the infinite balance trust fund also called the "Santa Claus Trust Fund Account" depends on it, or else the magic will disappear. If a naughty or not nice person used this account for an evil or a mean purpose, this would freeze the account. No pun intended. This account needs to remain unfrozen so that good things can continue to be operational for Santa Claus.

I, Titus Uno, Certified Public Accountant, Forensic Certified Public Accountant, and Chartered Global Management Accountant, will always remember the day that Santa Claus appeared to me and told me that I had been selected to be the Treasurer of the "Santa Claus Trust Fund Account." It had come to his attention that I was supposed to be Treasurer of several other organizations, but that other people had lied and cheated to become the Treasurer instead of me, Titus Uno, Certified Public Accountant, Forensic Certified Public Accountant, and Chartered Global Management Accountant, becoming those organizations' Treasurer. This was pretty much a done deal in becoming the Treasurer of the "Santa Claus Trust Fund Account", because who in their correct mind would turn down Santa Claus.

So that is how I, Titus Uno, Certified Public Accountant, Forensic Certified Public Accountant, and Chartered Global Management Accountant, became this organization's Treasurer. Of course the "Santa Claus Trust Fund Account" has expenditures that I have never seen on other financial statements other than the ones on the "Santa Claus Trust Fund Account" financial statements. These are unique and special accounts and sub-accounts that are in the "Santa Claus Trust Fund Account."

Now, we will get into the special accounting of this "Santa Claus Trust Fund Account." These expenditures include monies that will be spent for the following out of the "Santa Claus Trust Fund Account Number 1225" which has 22 Sub-Accounts: the Santa Claus Convention Sub-Account Number 1225.01, the Christmas Spirit Sub-Account Number 1225.02, the Christmas Secret Santa Clauses Sub-Account Number 1225.03, the Christmas Santa Letters Sub-Account Number 1225.04, the Santa Claus Bell Ringers for the Salvation Army Sub-Account Number 1225.05, the Christmas Eve Santa Claus Deliveries Sub-Account Number 1225.06, the Christmas Meals Sub-Account Number 1225.07, the Christmas Decorations Sub-Account0 Number 1225.08, the Christmas Candy Canes Sub-Account Number 1225.09, the Christmas Gingerbread House Sub-Account Number 1225.10, the Christmas Fruitcake Sub-Account Number 1225.11, the Christmas Ice-Skating Sub-Account Number 1225.12, the Christmas Parade with Santa Claus Sub-Account Number 1225.13, the Christmas Presents Sub-Account Number 1225.14, the Christmas Trees Sub-Account Number 1225.15, the Christmas Parties Sub-Account Number 1225.16, the Christmas Carolers Sub-Account Number 1225.17, the Christmas Church Bells Sub-Account Number 1225.18, the Christmas Mistletoe and the Magical Kiss Sub-Account Number 1225.19, the Christmas Snowman Sub-Account Number 1225.20, the Christmas Mall Santa Claus and the Picture with that Christmas Mall Santa Claus Sub-Account Number 1225.21, and the Christmas Miracles Sub-Account Number 1225.22. This is the most awesome set of financial statements that I, Titus Uno, Certified Public Accountant, Forensic Certified Public Accountant, and Chartered Global Management

Accountant, have ever seen in my life. You have to agree with me that this is the best Sub-Accounts that you have probably looked at or have seen, too.

Each of the above Sub-Accounts have to be accounted for even though the "Santa Claus Trust Fund Account" is an infinite Trust Fund Account in that it does not go down, unless something happens that is not used for the greater good for Christmas. As Treasurer I, Titus Uno, Certified Public Accountant, Forensic Certified Public Accountant, and Chartered Global Management Accountant, have to make sure that this account and all of the twenty-two sub-accounts are not abused. This is fairly easy to accomplish since magic is involved.

It sounds great to be able to work with Santa Claus in auditing the "Santa Claus Trust Fund Account Number 1225" which has 22 Sub-Accounts: the Santa Claus Convention Sub-Accounts. While I, Titus Uno, Certified Public Accountant, Forensic Certified Public Accountant, and Chartered Global Management Accountant, am doing this special audit, the rest of my Forensic Certified Public Accountant team, Drew Samson – the private investigator, Dena Hope – the computer programmer and hacker, Veronica Jackson – the scheduler, organizer, and item collector, Jack "Sheriff" Starr- CEO or Chief Executive Office, are taking time off, so that they can all spend time with their own families at Christmastime..

It is important that my team spends time with their family at Christmastime since my team has worked hard the entire year. Drew Samson, Dena Hope, Jack Starr, and Veronica Jackson have all decided to spend time with their families in different locations. Christmas is a time where families gather together and enjoy being around each other. Families are very important whether you are single, married, separated or divorced, orphaned, or widowed. I, Titus Uno, Certified Public Accountant, Forensic Certified Public Accountant, and Chartered Global

Management Accountant, remember when dad, mom, sister, and I would meet at my grandparent's house with all of the other family members to open Christmas gifts and spend time together for Christmas. That was so much fun. All of the parents would talk, all the children would play. Those afternoons would fly. Families are what life is about. That and being nice to others. My grandparents were always so sweet and nice to all their children, grandchildren, and great-grandchildren.

First, Drew Samson, the Private Investigator of the Forensic Certified Public Accountant team always enjoys going undercover to gather information for me to help me solve the case. Drew Samson has a beautiful wife, Jill Samson, and 2 children, Simon Samson, a boy, who is ten and Delilah Samson, a girl, who is 8. Drew Samson works hard to support his family, while having the flexibility to see his children in the activities. It is great that Drew Samson has this job and a family especially at Christmas.

Drew and Jill, and their children: Simon, and Delilah Samson have decided to spend Christmas with Drew's family in Nashville, Tennessee, United States of America. So, I say, "Merry Christmas in Nashville and enjoy the music, Samson Family." The Samson Family plans to go to the Grand Ole Opry. It is awesome to hear music in Nashville, Tennessee, United States of America. The Samson Family is happy to be able to go to the Grand Ole Opry.

Second, Dena Hope, the computer programmer and genius of the Forensic Certified Public Accountant team. Dena Hope is single because she spent her time working really hard. That is why Dena Hope is one of the best computer programmers in the world. Dena Hope dedicates all of her free time working on the computer.

Dena Hope is going to spend Christmas with her parents at her childhood home. On the Sunday closest to Christmas, she goes to church with her parents. It is awesome to spend as much time with your parents as you can. The older that you get, the more this statement makes sense. Enjoy every minute together that you can. Happy Thanksgiving, Dena Hope. You will be glad that you have spent every Christmas with your parents.

Third, Jack "Sheriff" Starr is the Chief Executive Officer of the Forensic Certified Public Accountant team. Jack Starr is a very happily married man. His wife is Jessica Starr. Jack and Jessica are happily married and have been married for Twenty-three wonderful years. They have 5 children: two boys, Jim Starr and Jeff Starr and 3 girls, Janet Starr, Jill Starr, and Joan Starr. Jack and Jessica, Jim, Jeff, Janet, Jill, and Joan Starr all get along with each other and the have fun spending time with each other. They always take an annual family vacation. Over the years they have been to Paris, London, Hawaii, Orlando, Rome, Sydney, Cairo, Rio, Tokyo, Toronto, New York, and Washington, D.C. Jack Starr believes that spending time with his family is his favorite thing to do.

Jack and Jessica, Jim, Jeff, Janet, Jill, and Joan Starr decided to Dallas, Texas, United States of America. The Starr Family plans to go to a Dallas Cowboy Football Game and to a college bowl game. Jack hopes that he can visit with some of the Dallas Cowboy players and get some autographs.

Fourth, Veronica Jackson, the scheduler, organizer, and item collector for the team. Without her the operations of my team would not be possible. Every team need an organizer and a go getter. Veronica Jackson sets up the meeting and makes sure that we get to that meet on time. Veronica Jackson always helps us appear to be great by keeping up punctual and organized.

Veronica Jackson, believe it or not, worked for the President of the United States as one of his secretaries.

Veronica Jackson is happily married to her husband, Carl Jackson for 24 years. They have a daughter, Rose Jackson that has just graduated from college with a Master's Degree in Accounting. Carl and Veronica Jackson are very proud of Rose Jackson. She already has a job at one of the Big 4 accounting firms in the United States of America. Becoming a successful Certified Public Accountant has always been the goal of Rose Jackson. Veronica Jackson has been training for the Certified Public Accountant Examination for years and especially while she was in college getting an education. I, Titus Uno, have promised Rose Jackson that I will help her in her important journey to become a Certified Public Accountant.

I, Titus Uno, know a of a current Certified Public Accountant that it took that Certified Public Accountant about 12 years after passing the tough Certified Public Accountant Examination to get a Certified Public Accountant's signature to become a Certified Public Accountant. That breaks my heart every time that I think of that great Certified Public Accountant. However, he is one of the most caring Certified Public Accountants that I, Titus Uno, know about. He is very friendly and is a philanthropist to several charities around the world. He conducts Certified Public Accountant work all over the world and improves people's lives all over the globe. That is what happens when someone has to work hard for everything. That Certified Public Accountant has developed the talent of tenacity. I think that Rose Jackson will develop the talent of tenacity and kindness. Rose Jackson will also be a friendly Certified Public Accountant like the world famous Certified Public Accountant that I mentioned earlier.

Veronica Jackson and her husband Carl Jackson along with their daughter Rose Jackson have all chosen Washington, District of Columbia, United States of America as their Christmas destination like the Jackson Family did for their Thanksgiving destination. The Jackson family might even visit the White House, again. That will bring back memories for Veronica Jackson. Have fun Veronica Jackson, you deserve your vacation with your family.

I am very pleased to allow my team to spend time with their families during Christmastime. Each of my Forensic Certified Public Accountant team seems to be very happy to have time off to rest and relax with them families during the Christmastime. My team should be rested and relaxed when they get back to the office after Christmas. Spending time with family and friends are very important to me, Titus Uno, Certified Public Accountant, Forensic Certified Public Accountant, and Chartered Global Management Accountant.

Santa Claus started a Christmas Santa Claus Convention Sub-Account Number 1225.01 as a part of the "Santa Claus Trust Fund Account Number 1225." This Santa Claus Convention, you guessed it, is made up of Santa Claus lookalikes or doppelgangers. This Christmas Santa Claus is only open to Santa Clauses that get a very special indentation. Once this invitation is read, it turns into snow. No Santa Claus invitee knows how or why they were chosen to attend this Santa Claus Convention, but there has never been a Santa Claus Convention invitee that has not accepted their invite. Every Santa Claus invite has been very jolly and nice when the magical sleigh arrives to take them to the site of the Christmas Santa Claus Convention. This year it is going to be in Greenland and Poland. There are going to be a record number of jolly and nice Santa Clauses this year thanks to the "Santa Claus Trust Fund Account" being made available to be used to spread Christmas Spirit during this Christmastime. It is great that this fund is available.

The purpose of the Christmas Santa Claus Convention Sub-Account Number 1225.01 is to allow the Christmas Santa Claus Convention to enable the Christmas Season to be as magical as it can by using the monies from this fund. These monies allow the Christmas Santa Claus Convention to be more effective because more training can be made available to all of the Santa Clauses. All of these Santa Clauses are prepared for any situation that can possibly happen.

Santa Clauses from all over the world are invited to attend the Christmas Santa Claus Convention every year to prepare each invitee to be the best Santa Claus that each Santa Claus can be for the children all over the world. These thousands of thousands of Santa Clauses are all over the Santa Claus Convention locations, Greenland and Poland, practicing every possible situation of Christmas that Santa

Claus has to be prepared for at Christmastime. This is an awesome situation to see all of these Santa Clauses when they assemble for the big meetings at the Great Assembly at the big auditorium.

Santa Claus does extensive research to make sure that an imposter does no attend the Santa Claus Convention. If that did happen, the "Santa Claus Trust Fund Account" would go down in value. That would definitely be bad if the infinite amount of kind money in the "Santa Claus Trust Fund Account" drops or is frozen. Most people think that infinite amount cannot be reduced or frozen , but several geniuses have proved that this is a false conclusion. It is a fact that any number no matter how large, can be reduces even by a microscopic number.

The Santa Claus Convention involves several Santa Claus training courses or classes to get all of the Santa Clauses ready for their time as Santa Claus with all of the children. This is very sweet and nice to watch. This training ranges from having the perfect Santa Claus smile, to performing the most amazing magic that will amaze all of the children and their parents. For example, every Santa Claus should be able to make an unhappy child into the most well behaved child while that child is visiting with Santa Claus. This does not always happen, as evidenced by some of the selfies with Santa Claus showing an unhappy child. Some child are just unaffected by the Santa Claus magic, but these children are still considered nice. Most of the children are well behaved, though.

The Santa Claus Suit is red with a big thick belt. The red suit has a white border on the edges. This suit is large in size because Santa Claus is a large jolly man. It is important that Santa Claus is large. Santa Claus is always large because Santa Claus likes to eat large portions of sweets. Santa Claus is a very nice person.

The Santa Claus Hat is a symbol in itself. When people see a Santa's hat, they think of everything that Santa Claus stands for, which is being nice and sharing kindness. The Santa Claus Hat completes the Santa Claus Suit.

The Santa Claus laugh is jolly and happy. Santa Claus thinks that everything is going to work out for the best and Santa Claus is always jolly.

The Santa Claus mustache and Beard is what children expect every Santa Claus to have on his face. The children try to pull Santa Claus' beard to see if it is real. Santa Claus always gives a jolly laugh.

The Santa Claus always has a magical attitude in that Santa Claus always maintains a sweet and cheerful attitude with every child no matter what happens. Santa Claus has to have the kindest disposition, no matter what happens.

The Santa Claus Chair that Santa Claus sits in to have all the children sit in Santa Claus's lap and tells Santa Claus what the child would like for Christmas. Santa Claus always enjoys hearing what every child wants for Christmas.

The picture with Santa Claus has to be great. Santa Claus always has a jolly face with the nicest smile and sense of Christmas Spirit that makes the children magically believe that everyone is nice and not on the naughty list.

As Treasurer of the "Santa Claus Trust Fund Account Number 1225", I, Titus Uno, Certified Public Accountant, Forensic Certified Public Accountant, and Chartered Global Management Accountant, have to make sure that this Sub-Account: the Santa Claus Convention Sub-Account Number 1225.01, is magically perfect and accurately accountable for the trustees of the "Santa Claus Trust Fund Number 1225."

The Santa Claus Convention Sub-Account Number 1225.01 of the "Santa Claus Trust Fund Account Number 1225" has to be approved by the Treasurer which happens to be me, Titus Uno, Certified Public Accountant, Forensic Certified Public Accountant, and Chartered Global Management Accountant. The factor of naughty or nice is what has to be evaluated in order for the "Santa Claus Trust Fund Account

Number 1225" to be able to continue to be useful to continue the Santa Claus Convention Sub-Account Number 1225.01. I, Titus Uno, Certified Public Accountant, Forensic Certified Public Accountant, and Chartered Global Management Accountant, get to work with Santa Claus, Mrs. Santa Claus, and the Head Elf that is under Mr. and Mrs. Santa Claus, and the Accountant Elf. Every Santa Claus that attends the Santa Claus Convention is evaluated to make sure that nice is accurately entered beside every Santa Claus that attends the Santa Claus Convention. If naughty is entered beside even just one Santa Claus that attends the Santa Claus Convention, then there is a problem. However, there has never been a naughty enter by any Santa Claus that attends the Santa Claus Convention. There is a very low possibility that naughty will ever be placed by a Santa Claus that attends the Santa Claus Convention. I, Titus Uno, Certified Public Accountant, Forensic Certified Public Accountant, and Chartered Global Management Accountant, have to make sure that the naughty is changed to nice so that the Santa Claus Convention Sub-Account Number 1225.01 of the "Santa Claus Trust Fund Account Number 1225" can continue to be used for good and not bad or for nice and not naughty.

Santa Claus started a Christmas Santa Claus Convention Sub-Account Number 1225.01 as a part of the "Santa Claus Trust Fund Account Number 1225." Santa Claus uses this Sub-Account to make sure that every Santa Claus is prepared for every possible situation that might arise. Every Santa Claus is individually trained to be the most perfect Santa Claus in every way possible in order to be able to assist in the following Sub-Account of the "Santa Claus Trust Fund Account Number 1225": the Christmas Spirit Sub-Account Number 1225.02, the Christmas Secret Santa Clauses Sub-Account Number 1225.03, the Christmas Santa Letters Sub-Account Number 1225.04, the Santa Claus Bell Ringers for the Salvation Army Sub-Account Number 1225.05, the Christmas Eve Santa Claus Deliveries Sub-Account Number 1225.06, the Christmas Meals Sub-Account Number 1225.07, the Christmas Decorations Sub-Account0 Number 1225.08, the Christmas Candy Canes Sub-Account Number 1225.09, the Christmas Gingerbread House Sub-Account Number 1225.10, the Christmas Fruitcake Sub-Account Number 1225.11, the

Christmas Ice-Skating Sub-Account Number 1225.12, the Christmas Parade with Santa Claus Sub-Account Number 1225.13, the Christmas Presents Sub-Account Number 1225.14, the Christmas Trees Sub-Account Number 1225.15, the Christmas Parties Sub-Account Number 1225.16, the Christmas Carolers Sub-Account Number 1225.17, the Christmas Church Bells Sub-Account Number 1225.18, the Christmas Mistletoe and the Magical Kiss Sub-Account Number 1225.19, the Christmas Snowman Sub-Account Number 1225.20, the Christmas Mall Santa Claus and the Picture with that Christmas Mall Santa Claus Sub-Account Number 1225.21, and the Christmas Miracles Sub-Account Number 1225.22.

Chapter 3 the Christmas Spirit

The Christmas Spirit Number 1225.02 is a Sub-Account of the "Santa Claus Trust Fund Account Number 1225." The Christmas Spirit has to be present in order for this "Santa Claus Trust Fund Account" to remain unchanged.

The purpose of the Christmas Spirit Number 1225.02 is to allow the Christmas Spirit to enable the Christmas Season to be as magical as it can by using the monies from this fund. These monies allow the Christmas Spirit to be more effective because Christmas Spirit can be made available to all of the Santa Clauses and everyone in the world. All of these Santa Clauses and people are filled with the Christmas Spirit especially around Christmastime all over the entire world.

Everyone knows what Christmas Spirit is, because when the Christmas Spirit is present the situation is magically perfect. It might be as simple as smiling at someone, opening the door for someone, performing a good deed for someone, sending a note to someone, saying "Thank you.", or being a "Secret Santa" even though it is not Christmas. Magic. People being nice to each other for no gain or reason.

It is very important to think of others at Christmastime. This act of human kindness helps to spread the spirit of Christmas. People act go out of their way to be nice to perfect strangers. Nice people becomes nicer and mean people becomes nice thus creating the awesome spirit of Christmas at Christmastime. It would be terrific if this would happen all through the year, not just at Christmastime. The spirit of Christmas is the sense of a nice action occurring that usually does not happen. It is almost as if it was magic.

As Treasurer of the "Santa Claus Trust Fund Account Number 1225", I, Titus Uno, Certified Public Accountant, Forensic Certified Public Accountant, and Chartered Global Management Accountant, have to make sure that this Sub-Account: the Christmas Spirit Sub-Account Number 1225.02, is magically perfect and accurately accountable for the trustees of the "Santa Claus Trust Fund Account Number 1225."

The Christmas Spirit Sub-Account Number 1225.02 of the "Santa Claus Trust Fund Account Number 1225" has to be approved by the Treasurer which happens to be me, Titus Uno, Certified Public Accountant, Forensic Certified Public Accountant, and Chartered Global Management Accountant. The factor of naughty or nice is what has to be evaluated in order for the "Santa Claus Trust Fund Account Number 1225" to be able to continue to be useful to continue the Christmas Spirit Sub-Account Number 1225.02. I, Titus Uno, Certified Public Accountant, Forensic Certified Public Accountant, and Chartered Global Management Accountant, get to work with Santa Claus, Mrs. Santa Claus, and the Head Elf that is under Mr. and Mrs. Santa Claus, and the Accountant Elf. Every Santa Claus's Christmas Spirit is evaluated to make sure that nice is accurately entered beside every Santa Claus that shows Christmas Spirit. If naughty is entered beside even just one Santa Claus that does not show any sign of Christmas Spirit, then there is a problem. However, there has never been a naughty enter by any Santa Claus that did not show great Christmas Spirit. There is a very low possibility that naughty will ever be placed by a Santa Claus that shows terrible Christmas Spirit. I, Titus Uno, Certified Public Accountant, Forensic Certified Public Accountant, and Chartered Global Management Accountant, have to make sure that the naughty is changed to nice so that the Christmas Spirit Sub-Account Number 1225.02 of the "Santa Claus Trust Fund Account Number 1225" can continue to be used for nice and not naughty or for good and not bad.

Santa Claus started a Christmas Spirit Number 1225.02 as a part of the "Santa Claus Trust Fund Account Number 1225." The Christmas Spirit Sub-Account Number 1225.02 is needed to be shown by everyone in the world, especially around Christmastime.

Chapter 4 the Christmas Secret Santa Clauses

The Christmas Secret Santa Clauses Sub-Account Number 1225.03 is a Sub-Account of the "Santa Claus Trust Fund Account Number 1225." The Christmas Secret Santa is a cool ways to show that everyone has a secret person that has thought of them. Someone pretends to be Santa and give someone a gift without that person knowing who got the present for that person. The group usually sets a range for gifts. There is usually at least one person that goes over budget, but someone else may not even get a gift for the person that they are supposed to get the present or gift for as secret Santa.

The purpose of the Christmas Secret Santa Clauses Sub-Account Number 1225.03 is to allow the Christmas Secret Santa to enable the Christmas Secret Santa to be as magical as it can by using the monies from this fund. These monies allow the Christmas Secret Santa to be more effective because more training can be made available to all of the Santa Clauses. All of these Secret Santa Clauses be able to give the most perfect gifts to the person that the Secret Santa Claus gives to gift to as the Secret Santa Claus. These gifts are given to the person from the Secret Santa Claus, not with the giver's true name on the gift tag.

Here comes Secret Santa Claus, here comes Secret Santa Claus with your secret Christmas gift. It is awesome to be the Secret Santa Claus and it is also great to be the Secret Santa Claus gift receiver. Someone gets something great to happen, but that person does not know who made this something happen or helps it work out for the best. It is amazing when someone says that something will not ever work out for the best, but somehow this event or action does work out for the best. It is as if a Secret Santa Claus worked their magic.

As Treasurer of the "Santa Claus Trust Fund Account Number 1225", I, Titus Uno, Certified Public Accountant, Forensic Certified Public Accountant, and Chartered Global Management Accountant, have to make sure that this Sub-Account: the Christmas Secret Santa Clauses Sub-Account Number 1225.03, is magically perfect and accurately accountable for the trustees of the "Santa Claus Trust Fund Account Number 1225."

The Christmas Secret Santa Clauses Sub-Account Number 1225.03 of the "Santa Claus Trust Fund Account Number 1225" has to be approved by the Treasurer which happens to be me, Titus Uno, Certified Public Accountant, Forensic Certified Public Accountant, and Chartered Global Management Accountant. The factor of naughty or nice is what has to be evaluated in order for the "Santa Claus Trust Fund Account Number 1225" to be able to continue to be useful to continue the Christmas Secret Santa Clauses Sub-Account Number 1225.03. I, Titus Uno, Certified Public Accountant, Forensic Certified Public Accountant, and Chartered Global Management Accountant, get to work with Santa Claus, Mrs. Santa Claus, and the Head Elf that is under Mr. and Mrs. Santa Claus, and the Accountant Elf. Every Santa Claus that helps other Christmas Secret Santa Clauses is evaluated to make sure that nice is accurately entered beside every Santa Claus that helps other Christmas Secret Santa Clauses. If naughty is entered beside even just one Santa Claus that helps other Christmas Secret Santa Clauses, then there is a problem. However, there has never been a naughty enter by any Santa Claus that has helped other Christmas Secret Santa Clauses. There is a very low possibility that naughty will ever be placed by a Santa Claus that has helped other Christmas Secret Santa Clauses. I, Titus Uno, Certified Public Accountant, Forensic Certified Public Accountant, and Chartered Global Management Accountant, have to make sure that the naughty is changed to nice so that the Santa Clauses that have helped in the Christmas Secret Santa Clauses Sub-Account Number 1225.03 of the "Santa Claus Clauses Trust Fund Account Number 1225" can continue to be used for good and not bad or for nice and not naughty.

Santa Claus started a Christmas Secret Santa Clauses Sub-Account Number 1225.03 as a part of the

"Santa Claus Trust Fund Account Number 1225." Christmas Secret Santa Clauses

The Christmas Santa Letters Sub-Account Number 1225.04 is a Sub-Account of the "Santa Claus Trust Fund Account Number 1225."

The purpose of the Christmas Santa Letters Sub-Account Number 1225.04 is to allow the Christmas Santa Letters to enable the Christmas Season to be as magical as it can by using the monies from this fund. These monies allow the Christmas Santa Letters to be more effective because Santa Clauses needs to know what all of the Christmas Santa Letter writers would like for Christmas. All of these Santa Claus' Letter are written with love from all of the children from all over the world.

Dear Santa Claus Letters have to make it to Santa Claus at the North Pole. In fact, every Santa Claus Letter does make it to the North Pole, even if it takes magic. It is amazing that Santa Claus knows what every child wants for Christmas. Every child knows that they need to be good or nice to get their presents. The children's letters are sent to Santa Claus in an envelope addressed as follows:

Child's Name   **STAMP**

Child's Address   **HERE**

Child's City, State, Zip Code

Santa Claus

North Pole

The post offices everywhere makes sure that these letters are sent to Santa Claus at the North Pole, so that Santa Claus will have a record of what every child wants. Every child enjoys sending Santa Claus a Christmas Letter. It is great when the child gets what that child writes to Santa Claus in the letter. The child is so excited while writing Santa Claus.

As Treasurer of the "Santa Claus Trust Fund Account Number 1225", I, Titus Uno, Certified Public Accountant, Forensic Certified Public Accountant, and Chartered Global Management Accountant, have to make sure that this Sub-Account: the Christmas Santa Letters Sub-Account Number 1225.04, is magically perfect and accurately accountable for the trustees of the "Santa Claus Trust Fund Account Number 1225."

The Christmas Santa Letters Sub-Account Number 1225.04 of the "Santa Claus Trust Fund Account Number 1225" has to be approved by the Treasurer which happens to be me, Titus Uno, Certified Public Accountant, Forensic Certified Public Accountant, and Chartered Global Management Accountant. The factor of naughty or nice is what has to be evaluated in order for the "Santa Claus Trust Fund Account Number 1225" to be able to continue to be useful to continue the Christmas Santa Letters Sub-Account Number 1225.04. I, Titus Uno, Certified Public Accountant, Forensic Certified Public Accountant, and Chartered Global Management Accountant, get to work with Santa Claus, Mrs. Santa Claus, and the Head Elf that is under Mr. and Mrs. Santa Claus, and the Accountant Elf. Every Santa Claus that assists in the Christmas Santa Letters is evaluated to make sure that nice is accurately entered beside every Santa Claus that participates in the Christmas Santa Letters Sub-Account Number 1225.04. If naughty is entered beside even just one Santa Claus that participates in the Christmas Santa Letters Sub-Account Number 1225.04, then there is a problem. However, there has never been a naughty enter by any Santa Claus that participates in the Christmas Santa Letters Sub-Account Number 1225.04. There is a very low possibility that naughty will ever be placed by a Santa Claus that participates in the Christmas Santa Letters Sub-Account Number 1225.04. I , Titus Uno, Certified Public Accountant, Forensic Certified Public Accountant, and Chartered Global Management Accountant, have to make sure that the naughty is changed to nice so that the Christmas Santa Letters Sub-Account Number 1225.04 of the "Santa Claus

Trust Fund Account Number 1225" can continue to be used for nice and not naughty or for good and not bad.

Santa Claus started a Christmas Santa Letters Sub-Account Number 1225.04 as a part of the "Santa Claus Trust Fund Account Number 1225."

The Santa Claus Bell Ringers for the Salvation Army Sub-Account Number 1225.05 is a Sub-Account of the "Santa Claus Trust Fund Account Number 1225."

The purpose of the Santa Claus Bell Ringers for the Salvation Army Sub-Account Number 1225.05 is to allow the Santa Claus Bell Ringers for the Salvation Army to enable the Christmas Season to be as magical as it can by using the monies from this fund. These monies allow the Santa Claus Bell Ringers for the Salvation Army to be more effective because more Santa Claus can be made available to ring the bells. All of these Santa Clauses are prepared to ring those bells.

The Christmas Santa Claus Bell Ringers are an important part of the Christmas Season. The monies raised are used to buy toys and gifts for parents that need help to buy toy for their children. Every child needs to have toys and clothes for Christmas. Every Santa Claus is excited and willing to help the Salvation Army ring those precious bells. As these Christmas Santa Clauses ring the bells as customers enter and exit the store, customers are willing to contribute to the Santa Claus Bell Ringers for the Salvation Army by put the monies into the pot that is setup for the customer's contribution. Ring, ring, ring. Thank you, for your contribution. Merry Christmas.

Every cent that is collected helps to make a child's Christmas better by making it possible for that child to get clothes and toys. Every child needs to be happy at Christmastime. It is impossible for Santa Claus to imagine a child with a Christmas toy or clothes. That is why every Santa Claus works so hard to raise as much money as the Christmas Santa Claus can raise. The Santa Claus rings and rings and rings those Christmas Salvation Army Bells for the sweet and nice children.

As Treasurer of the "Santa Claus Trust Fund Account Number 1225", I, Titus Uno, Certified Public Accountant, Forensic Certified Public Accountant, and Chartered Global Management Accountant, have to make sure that this Sub-Account: the Santa Claus Bell Ringers for the Salvation Army Sub-Account Number 1225.05, is magically perfect and accurately accountable for the trustees of the "Santa Claus Trust Fund Account Number 1225."

The Santa Claus Bell Ringers for the Salvation Army Sub-Account Number 1225.05 of the "Santa Claus Trust Fund Account Number 1225" has to be approved by the Treasurer which happens to be me, Titus Uno, Certified Public Accountant, Forensic Certified Public Accountant, and Chartered Global Management Accountant. The factor of naughty or nice is what has to be evaluated in order for the "Santa Claus Trust Fund Account Number 1225" to be able to continue to be useful to continue the Santa Claus Bell Ringers for the Salvation Army Sub-Account Number 1225.05. I, Titus Uno, Certified Public Accountant, Forensic Certified Public Accountant, and Chartered Global Management Accountant, get to work with Santa Claus, Mrs. Santa Claus, and the Head Elf that is under Mr. and Mrs. Santa Claus, and the Accountant Elf. Every Santa Claus that attends the Santa Claus Convention is evaluated to make sure that nice is accurately entered beside every Santa Claus that participates in the Santa Claus Bell Ringers for the Salvation Army Sub-Account Number 1225.05. If naughty is entered beside even just one Santa Claus that participates in the Santa Claus Bell Ringers for the Salvation Army Sub-Account Number 1225.05, then there is a problem. However, there has never been a naughty enter by any Santa Claus that has participated in the Santa Claus Bell Ringers for the Salvation Army Sub-Account Number 1225.05. There is a very low possibility that naughty will ever be placed by a Santa Claus that participates in the Santa Claus Bell Ringers for the Salvation Army Sub-Account Number 1225.05. I, Titus Uno, Certified Public Accountant, Forensic Certified Public Accountant, and Chartered Global Management Accountant, have to make sure that the naughty is changed to nice so that the

Santa Claus Bell Ringers for the Salvation Army Sub-Account Number 1225.05 of the "Santa Claus Trust Fund Account Number 1225" can continue to be used for good and not bad or for nice and not naughty.

Santa Claus started a Santa Claus Bell Ringers for the Salvation Army Sub-Account Number 1225.05 as a part of the "Santa Claus Trust Fund Account Number 1225."

Chapter 7 the Christmas Eve Santa Claus Deliveries

The Christmas Eve Santa Claus Deliveries Sub-Account Number 1225.06 is a Sub-Account of the "Santa Claus Trust Fund Account Number 1225."

The purpose of the Christmas Eve Santa Claus Deliveries Sub-Account Number 1225.06 is to allow the Christmas Eve Santa Claus Deliveries to enable the Christmas Season to be as magical as it can by using the monies from this fund. These monies allow the Christmas Eve Santa Claus Deliveries to be more effective because more training can be made available to all of the Santa Clauses to be able to deliver all of the children's gifts for being nice and kind all year. All of these Santa Clauses are prepared for any situation that can possibly happen while delivering the gifts to all of the children all over the world.

On Christmas Eve Santa Claus goes on his journey to deliver the gifts to all of the good children all over the world. Santa Claus has the best gadgets available to him so that all of the children's gifts can be delivered as easily as possible. The elves are always working on new technology gadgets for Santa Claus to make his journey safer and more efficient. The elves also work on gadgets to help Mrs. Claus to keep her happy. Mr. and Mrs. Santa Claus are always happy.

The magical reindeer what makes Santa Claus's Sleigh fly up into the sky. One of the magical reindeer has a red nose to guide the sleigh. These reindeer are very famous because they all help to guide Santa Claus's Sleigh so that all of the children in the world can get their gifts. If all the children in the world do not get their gifts that would not be nice.

The sleigh is loaded with gadgets to help Santa Claus. Santa Claus needs to be comfortable as he goes from house to house to house to house. Santa Claus's Sleigh has improved so much over the years. The ride is so smooth that Santa Claus can eat his cookies and drink his milk without spilling any of his

Christmas Treats.

The Santa Claus Sack is magically filled with gifts that should not be able to fit inside the Santa Claus

sack. This beautiful sack or bag is so elegant and matches Santa Claus's Suit. This Santa Claus Sack is

what makes carrying the toys from the Santa Claus Sleigh to the child's Christmas Tree as soon as

possible.

The cookies and milk are Santa Claus's favorite food because it tastes great and it shows Santa Claus

that children loves Santa Claus. This always makes Santa Claus smile and laugh his jolly laugh.

As Treasurer of the "Santa Claus Trust Fund Account Number 1225", I, Titus Uno, Certified Public

Accountant, Forensic Certified Public Accountant, and Chartered Global Management Accountant, have

to make sure that this Sub-Account: the Christmas Eve Santa Claus Deliveries Sub-Account Number

1225.06, is magically perfect and accurately accountable for the trustees of the "Santa Claus Trust Fund

Account Number 1225."

The Christmas Eve Santa Claus Deliveries Sub-Account Number 1225.06 of the "Santa Claus Trust

Fund Account Number 1225" has to be approved by the Treasurer which happens to be me, Titus Uno,

Certified Public Accountant, Forensic Certified Public Accountant, and Chartered Global Management

Accountant. The factor of naughty or nice is what has to be evaluated in order for the "Santa Claus Trust

Fund Account Number 1225" to be able to continue to be useful to continue the Christmas Eve Santa

Claus Deliveries Sub-Account Number 1225.06. I, Titus Uno, Certified Public Accountant, Forensic

Certified Public Accountant, and Chartered Global Management Accountant, get to work with Santa

Claus, Mrs. Santa Claus, and the Head Elf that is under Mr. and Mrs. Santa Claus, and the Accountant Elf.

Every Santa Claus that attends the Santa Claus Convention is evaluated to make sure that nice is

accurately entered beside every Santa Claus that helps with the Christmas Eve Santa Claus Deliveries

Sub-Account Number 1225.06. If naughty is entered beside even just one Santa Claus that helps with the Christmas Eve Santa Claus Deliveries Sub-Account Number 1225.06, then there is a problem. However, there has never been a naughty enter by any Santa Claus that helps with the Christmas Eve Santa Claus Deliveries Sub-Account Number 1225.06. There is a very low possibility that naughty will ever be placed by a Santa Claus that helps with the Christmas Eve Santa Claus Deliveries Sub-Account Number 1225.06. I , Titus Uno, Certified Public Accountant, Forensic Certified Public Accountant, and Chartered Global Management Accountant, have to make sure that the naughty is changed to nice so that the Christmas Eve Santa Claus Deliveries Sub-Account Number 1225.06 of the "Santa Claus Trust Fund Account Number 1225" can continue to be used for nice and not naughty or for good and not bad.

Santa Claus started a Christmas Eve Santa Claus Deliveries Sub-Account Number 1225.06 as a part of the "Santa Claus Trust Fund Account Number 1225."

The Christmas Meals Sub-Account Number 1225.07 is a Sub-Account of the "Santa Claus Trust Fund Account Number 1225."

The purpose of the Christmas Meals Sub-Account Number 1225.07 is to allow the Christmas Meals to enable the Christmas Season to be as magical as it can by using the monies from this fund. These monies allow the Christmas Meals Sub to be more effective because more training can be made available to all of the Santa Clauses and other nice and kind people to make and deliver Christmas Meals all over the world. All of these Santa Clauses are prepared for any situation that can possibly happen while delivering Christmas all over the world.

Serving meals to the homeless or to people that cannot prepare Thanksgiving meals for them self is so great to do around Christmastime. It is evident that the people that are served these meals are very appreciative of this act of selfless kindness, goodness or being nice.

People go out of their way to help serve Christmas meals to those that need help get a Christmas meal. Christmas meals are so important because it helps hungry people have a special Christmas meal for Christmastime. Serving these Christmas meals shows that nice people care about those that need help to get a special Christmas meal for Christmastime.

Churches and other organizations go all out with fundraising to fund the Christmas meals. These meals are sometimes delivered on wheels to people that cannot get out to eat the Christmas Meals and cannot prepare their own meals. These meals are necessary to help everyone to have a great Christmas Meal at Christmastime and to possibly have the only company that the Christmas Meal recipient will have at Christmastime. The Christmas Meal preparer, deliverer, and the Christmas Meal recipient are all the recipient of having a better Christmas because of the Christmas Meal Sub-Account Number 1225.07 of the "Santa Claus Trust Fund Account Number 1225."

As Treasurer of the "Santa Claus Trust Fund Account Number 1225", I, Titus Uno, Certified Public Accountant, Forensic Certified Public Accountant, and Chartered Global Management Accountant, have to make sure that this Sub-Account: the Christmas Meals Sub-Account Number 1225.07, is magically perfect and accurately accountable for the trustees of the "Santa Claus Trust Fund Account Number 1225."

The Christmas Meals Sub-Account Number 1225.07 of the "Santa Claus Trust Fund Account Number 1225" has to be approved by the Treasurer which happens to be me, Titus Uno, Certified Public Accountant, Forensic Certified Public Accountant, and Chartered Global Management Accountant. The factor of naughty or nice is what has to be evaluated in order for the "Santa Claus Trust Fund Account Number 1225" to be able to continue to be useful to continue the Christmas Meals Sub-Account Number 1225.07. I, Titus Uno, Certified Public Accountant, Forensic Certified Public Accountant, and Chartered Global Management Accountant, get to work with Santa Claus, Mrs. Santa Claus, and the Head Elf that is under Mr. and Mrs. Santa Claus, and the Accountant Elf. Every Santa Claus that helps with the Christmas Meals Sub-Account Number 1225.07 is evaluated to make sure that nice is accurately entered beside every Santa Claus that helps with the Christmas Meals Sub-Account Number 1225.07. If naughty is entered beside even just one Santa Claus that helps with the Christmas Meals Sub-Account Number 1225.07, then there is a problem. However, there has never been a naughty enter by any Santa Claus that helps with the Christmas Meals Sub-Account Number 1225.07. There is a very low possibility that naughty will ever be placed by a Santa Claus that helps with the Christmas Meals Sub-Account Number 1225.07. I, Titus Uno, Certified Public Accountant, Forensic Certified Public Accountant, and Chartered Global Management Accountant, have to make sure that the naughty is changed to nice so that the Christmas Meals Sub-Account Number 1225.07 of the "Santa Claus Trust Fund Account Number 1225" can continue to be used for good and not bad or for nice and not naughty.

Santa Claus started a Christmas Meals Sub-Account Number 1225.07 as a part of the "Santa Claus Trust Fund Account Number 1225."

The Christmas Decorations Sub-Account Number 1225.08 is a Sub-Account of the "Santa Claus Trust Fund Account Number 1225."

The purpose of the Christmas Decorations Sub-Account Number 1225.08 is to allow the Christmas Decorations to enable the Christmas Season to be as magical as it can by using the monies from this fund. These monies allow the Christmas Decorations to be more effective because more training can be made available to all of the Santa Clauses and other nice and kind people to set up Christmas Decorations for themselves and for others. All of these Santa Clauses are prepared for any situation that can possibly happen while setting up the Christmas Decorations.

Families enjoy decorating their houses and yards. Most families put up Christmas Lights on their house to show other people that pass their house that the family in this house has the Christmas Spirit. Some of these Christmas lights are simple while other Christmas lights are very complicated and even flash on and off to music.

Businesses decorate their office spaces for Christmas time. Some businesses go all out and decorate their businesses with expensive decorations that even include the business name on these Christmas decorations.

Cities often decorate city properties. Most cities spend funds to have humongous decorations so that people that pass the city can get some of that city's Christmas Spirit. These decorations are very important to the cities that put up these Christmas decorations. Some of these decorations are very large and make the city's citizens and visitors get the Christmas Spirit in their heart because of these decorations are so pretty and cause the city's citizens and visitors to remember some past special person or event.

As Treasurer of the "Santa Claus Trust Fund Account Number 1225", I, Titus Uno, Certified Public Accountant, Forensic Certified Public Accountant, and Chartered Global Management Accountant, have to make sure that this Sub-Account: the Christmas Decorations Sub-Account Number 1225.08, is magically perfect and accurately accountable for the trustees of the "Santa Claus Trust Fund Account Number 1225."

The Christmas Decorations Sub-Account Number 1225.08 of the "Santa Claus Trust Fund Account Number 1225" has to be approved by the Treasurer which happens to be me, Titus Uno, Certified Public Accountant, Forensic Certified Public Accountant, and Chartered Global Management Accountant. The factor of naughty or nice is what has to be evaluated in order for the "Santa Claus Trust Fund Account Number 1225" to be able to continue to be useful to continue the Christmas Decorations Sub-Account Number 1225.08. I, Titus Uno, Certified Public Accountant, Forensic Certified Public Accountant, and Chartered Global Management Accountant, get to work with Santa Claus, Mrs. Santa Claus, and the Head Elf that is under Mr. and Mrs. Santa Claus, and the Accountant Elf. Every Santa Claus that helps with the Christmas Decorations Sub-Account Number 1225.08 is evaluated to make sure that nice is accurately entered beside every Santa Claus that helps with the Christmas Decorations Sub-Account Number 1225.08. If naughty is entered beside even just one Santa Claus that helps with the Christmas Decorations Sub-Account Number 1225.08, then there is a problem. However, there has never been a naughty enter by any Santa Claus that helps with the Christmas Decorations Sub-Account Number 1225.08. There is a very low possibility that naughty will ever be placed by a Santa Claus that helps with the Christmas Decorations Sub-Account Number 1225.08. I , Titus Uno, Certified Public Accountant, Forensic Certified Public Accountant, and Chartered Global Management Accountant, have to make sure that the naughty is changed to nice so that the Christmas Decorations Sub-Account Number 1225.08 of the "Santa Claus Trust Fund Account Number 1225" can continue to be used for nice and not naughty or for good and not bad.

Santa Claus started a Christmas Decorations Sub-Account Number 1225.08 as a part of the "Santa Claus Trust Fund Account Number 1225."

Chapter 10 the Christmas Candy Canes

The Christmas Candy Canes Sub-Account Number 1225.09 is a Sub-Account of the "Santa Claus Trust Fund Account Number 1225."

The purpose of the Christmas Candy Canes Sub-Account Number 1225.09 is to allow the Christmas Candy Canes to enable the Christmas Season to be as magical as it can by using the monies from this fund. These monies allow the Christmas Candy Canes to be more effective because more training can be made available to all of the Santa Clauses to hand out more Christmas Candy Canes and to make more Christmas Candy Canes decorations. All of these Santa Clauses are prepared for any situation that can possibly happen while preparing all of the Christmas Candy Canes.

Christmas Candy Canes are an important part of Christmas. These Christmas Candy Canes are a Christmas staple for most families at Christmastime. These Christmas Candy Canes can be put on cups of apple cider, hot cocoa, egg nog, or hot coffee. The shape of the Christmas Candy Canes makes it perfect to be hooked on items such as tables, cups, or Christmas Trees.

Most Christmas Candy Canes are white with red stripes and tastes like regular peppermints. However, Christmas Candy Canes can be made in different colors and different flavors. No matter the color are flavor these Christmas Candy Canes make everyone think of Christmas and sometimes even a special event or person. This is part of what makes Christmas special. It is great to have individually wrapped Christmas Candy Canes out so that people that pass by the bowl of Christmas Candy Canes can pick one up and enjoy the magic of the Christmas Candy Cane.

Christmas Candy Canes are in the shape of canes and in the shape of shepherd staffs. The shape of the Christmas Candy Canes helps people to think of Christmastime.

There is something special about eating a Christmas Candy Cane at Christmastime. Peppermint is great tasting and sometimes it helps to sooth a sore or scratchy throat. Plus a Christmas Candy Cane is just a Christmas item.

As Treasurer of the "Santa Claus Trust Fund Account Number 1225", I, Titus Uno, Certified Public Accountant, Forensic Certified Public Accountant, and Chartered Global Management Accountant, have to make sure that this Sub-Account: the Christmas Candy Canes Sub-Account Number 1225.09, is magically perfect and accurately accountable for the trustees of the "Santa Claus Trust Fund Account Number 1225."

The Christmas Candy Canes Sub-Account Number 1225.09 of the "Santa Claus Trust Fund Account Number 1225" has to be approved by the Treasurer which happens to be me, Titus Uno, Certified Public Accountant, Forensic Certified Public Accountant, and Chartered Global Management Accountant. The factor of naughty or nice is what has to be evaluated in order for the "Santa Claus Trust Fund Account Number 1225" to be able to continue to be useful to continue the Christmas Candy Canes Sub-Account Number 1225.09. I, Titus Uno, Certified Public Accountant, Forensic Certified Public Accountant, and Chartered Global Management Accountant, get to work with Santa Claus, Mrs. Santa Claus, and the Head Elf that is under Mr. and Mrs. Santa Claus, and the Accountant Elf. Every Santa Claus that helps with the Christmas Candy Canes Sub-Account Number 1225.09 is evaluated to make sure that nice is accurately entered beside every Santa Claus that helps with the Christmas Candy Canes Sub-Account Number 1225.09. If naughty is entered beside even just one Santa Claus that helps with the Christmas Candy Canes Sub-Account Number 1225.09, then there is a problem. However, there has never been a naughty enter by any Santa Claus that helps with the Christmas Candy Canes Sub-Account Number 1225.09. There is a very low possibility that naughty will ever be placed by a Santa Claus that helps with the Christmas Candy Canes Sub-Account Number 1225.09. I, Titus Uno, Certified Public Accountant, Forensic Certified Public Accountant, and Chartered Global Management Accountant, have to make sure that the naughty is changed to nice so that the Christmas Candy Canes Sub-Account Number 1225.09 of the "Santa Claus Trust Fund Account Number 1225" can continue to be used for good and not bad or for nice and not naughty.

Santa Claus started a Christmas Candy Canes Sub-Account Number 1225.09 as a part of the "Santa Claus Trust Fund Account Number 1225."

Chapter 11 the Christmas Gingerbread House

The Christmas Gingerbread House Sub-Account Number 1225.10 is a Sub-Account of the "Santa Claus Trust Fund Account Number 1225."

The purpose of the Christmas Gingerbread House Sub-Account Number 1225.10 is to allow the Christmas Gingerbread House to enable the Christmas Season to be as magical as it can by using the monies from this fund. These monies allow the Christmas Gingerbread House to be more effective because more training can be made available to all of the Santa Clauses to help assist in the building of the Christmas Gingerbread Houses. All of these Santa Clauses are prepared for any situation that can possibly happen in the building of the Christmas Gingerbread Houses.

Christmas Gingerbread Houses are very fun to cook, make, build, and decorated as a family activity. All of these steps have to be performed in order to have a completed Christmas Gingerbread House.

Christmas Gingerbread Houses are fun to cook or bake. The Christmas Gingerbread House gingerbread has to be baked or bought.

Christmas Gingerbread Houses are fun to make. The Christmas Gingerbread House shape or pattern has to be cut out in order to get the shapes that are needed.

Christmas Gingerbread Houses are fun to build. The cut out shapes from above have to be assembled in order to get the Gingerbread House shape.

Christmas Gingerbread Houses are fun to decorate. Once the Christmas Gingerbread House is shaped and built, the Christmas Gingerbread House has to be decorated with candy and icing. Most of these Christmas Gingerbread Houses are decorated with sweet candy and white icing to represent the snow that is usually on real houses at Christmastime.

Christmas Gingerbread Houses are a great Christmas Family Tradition because it takes so much time to arrive at a completed Christmas Gingerbread House. When a Christmas Gingerbread House is completed, a family can say that the family has accomplished something special together.

As Treasurer of the "Santa Claus Trust Fund Account Number 1225", I, Titus Uno, Certified Public Accountant, Forensic Certified Public Accountant, and Chartered Global Management Accountant, have to make sure that this Sub-Account: the Christmas Gingerbread House Sub-Account Number 1225.10, is magically perfect and accurately accountable for the trustees of the "Santa Claus Trust Fund Account Number 1225."

The Christmas Gingerbread House Sub-Account Number 1225.10 of the "Santa Claus Trust Fund Account Number 1225" has to be approved by the Treasurer which happens to be me, Titus Uno, Certified Public Accountant, Forensic Certified Public Accountant, and Chartered Global Management Accountant. The factor of naughty or nice is what has to be evaluated in order for the "Santa Claus Trust Fund Account Number 1225" to be able to continue to be useful to continue the Christmas Gingerbread House Sub-Account Number 1225.10. I, Titus Uno, Certified Public Accountant, Forensic Certified Public Accountant, and Chartered Global Management Accountant, get to work with Santa Claus, Mrs. Santa Claus, and the Head Elf that is under Mr. and Mrs. Santa Claus, and the Accountant Elf. Every Santa Claus that helps with the Christmas Gingerbread House Sub-Account Number 1225.10 is evaluated to make sure that nice is accurately entered beside every Santa Claus that helps with the Christmas Gingerbread House Sub-Account Number 1225.10. If naughty is entered beside even just one Santa Claus that helps with the Christmas Gingerbread House Sub-Account Number 1225.10, then there is a problem. However, there has never been a naughty enter by any Santa Claus that helps with the Christmas Gingerbread House Sub-Account Number 1225.10. There is a very low possibility that naughty will ever be placed by a Santa Claus that helps with the Christmas Gingerbread House Sub-Account Number 1225.10. I , Titus Uno, Certified Public Accountant, Forensic Certified Public

Accountant, and Chartered Global Management Accountant, have to make sure that the naughty is changed to nice so that the Christmas Gingerbread House Sub-Account Number 1225.10 of the "Santa Claus Trust Fund Account Number 1225" can continue to be used for nice and not naughty or for good and not bad.

Santa Claus started a Christmas Gingerbread House Sub-Account Number 1225.10 as a part of the "Santa Claus Trust Fund Account Number 1225."

Chapter 12 the Christmas Fruitcake

The Christmas Fruitcake Sub-Account Number 1225.11 is a Sub-Account of the "Santa Claus Trust Fund Account Number 1225."

The purpose of the Christmas Fruitcake Sub-Account Number 1225.11 is to allow the Christmas Fruitcake Sub-Account to enable the Christmas Season to be as magical as it can by using the monies from this fund. These monies allow the Christmas Fruitcake Sub-Account to be more effective because more training can be made available to all of the Santa Clauses to help assist in the baking of the Christmas Fruitcakes. All of these Santa Clauses are prepared for any situation that can possibly happen in the baking of the Christmas Fruitcake to be distributed to everyone at Christmastime.

Christmas Fruitcakes are very fun to give as gifts. All of these fruitcakes have to be given out to family members and friends in order to have a funny Christmas. A Christmas is not complete until you give or get a Christmas Fruitcake at Christmastime. Some people joke that there is only one Christmas Fruitcake in the entire world and that it is passed from one person to another. This is definitely only a joke because there are millions of Christmas Fruitcakes that are available all over the world to be given as Christmas Gifts. These Christmas Fruitcakes do actually make great gifts for desserts. These Christmas Fruitcakes are rich cakes that include candied fruit. These Christmas Fruitcakes are very delicious to eat at Christmastime. The Christmas Fruitcake Sub-Account Number 1225.11 is a Sub-Account of the "Santa Claus Trust Fund Account Number 1225" help to make Christmastime better for the Christmas Fruitcake giver and for the Christmas Fruitcake receiver. Both the Christmas Fruitcake giver and the Christmas Fruitcake receiver can enjoy the Christmas Fruitcake together along with everyone else that is present when the Christmas Fruitcake is presented and is opened by the Christmas Fruitcake recipient.

Some people buy their Christmas Fruitcakes while other people make their own Christmas Fruitcakes in order to give as Christmas Gifts to their family, to their friends, to their bosses, or even to their co-workers.

As Treasurer of the "Santa Claus Trust Fund Account Number 1225", I, Titus Uno, Certified Public Accountant, Forensic Certified Public Accountant, and Chartered Global Management Accountant, have to make sure that this Sub-Account: the Christmas Fruitcake Sub-Account Number 1225.11, is magically perfect and accurately accountable for the trustees of the "Santa Claus Trust Fund Account Number 1225."

The Christmas Fruitcake Sub-Account Number 1225.11 of the "Santa Claus Trust Fund Account Number 1225" has to be approved by the Treasurer which happens to be me, Titus Uno, Certified Public Accountant, Forensic Certified Public Accountant, and Chartered Global Management Accountant. The factor of naughty or nice is what has to be evaluated in order for the "Santa Claus Trust Fund Account Number 1225" to be able to continue to be useful to continue the Christmas Fruitcake Sub-Account Number 1225.11. I, Titus Uno, Certified Public Accountant, Forensic Certified Public Accountant, and Chartered Global Management Accountant, get to work with Santa Claus, Mrs. Santa Claus, and the Head Elf that is under Mr. and Mrs. Santa Claus, and the Accountant Elf. Every Santa Claus that helps with the Christmas Fruitcake Sub-Account Number 1225.11 is evaluated to make sure that nice is accurately entered beside every Santa Claus that helps with the Christmas Fruitcake Sub-Account Number 1225.11. If naughty is entered beside even just one Santa Claus that helps with the Christmas Fruitcake Sub-Account Number 1225.11, then there is a problem. However, there has never been a naughty enter by any Santa Claus that helps with the Christmas Fruitcake Sub-Account Number 1225.11. There is a very low possibility that naughty will ever be placed by a Santa Claus that helps with the Christmas Fruitcake Sub-Account Number 1225.11. I, Titus Uno, Certified Public Accountant, Forensic Certified Public Accountant, and Chartered Global Management Accountant, have to make sure that the naughty is changed to nice so that the Christmas Fruitcake Sub-Account Number 1225.11 of the "Santa Claus Trust Fund Account Number 1225" can continue to be used for nice and not naughty or for good and not bad.

Chapter 13 the Christmas Ice-Skating Rink

The Christmas Ice-Skating Sub-Account Number 1225.12 is a Sub-Account of the "Santa Claus Trust Fund Account Number 1225."

The purpose of the Christmas Ice-Skating Sub-Account Number 1225.12 is to allow the Christmas Ice-Skating Sub-Account to enable the Christmas Season to be as magical as it can by using the monies from this fund. These monies allow the Christmas Ice-Skating Sub-Account to be more effective because more training can be made available to all of the Santa Clauses and to help ice-skaters skate. All of these Santa Clauses are prepared for any situation that can possibly happen when Christmas Ice-Skaters skate.

Ice-Skating is a Christmas activity. It is very cool to go Christmas Ice-Skating, both figurative and literary. It is great exercise and is fun to do with your family or with a close friend. The Christmas Ice-Skating Sub-Account Number 1225.12 is a Sub-Account of the "Santa Claus Trust Fund Account Number 1225" is important in order to help improve the ice-skater's experience as the ice-skaters skate in the ice-skating rinks or frozen outdoor rinks or outdoor frozen ponds that are open at Christmastime all over the world. These Ice-Skating Rinks or frozen ponds allow ice-skaters from all over the world to ice-skate to Christmas Music and to possibly view pretty Christmas Decorations that have been placed out so that the ice-skaters can view the Christmas Decorations and hear the Christmas Music as the ice-skaters skate. It is so fun to ice-skate with family and friends. This is even a great Christmas activity that people that are dating can do as a date. This might even lead to their getting married to each other and become one of the wedding anniversary's remembrance stories that that couple always tells. For example that couple might say, "We may never have gotten married, if we had not gone Ice-Skating at Christmastime with each other." That is very important for single people to have things to do with other single people that are their age. Churches should also help in this area to help single career people meet

each other in a nice environment. I, Titus Uno, Certified Public Accountant, Forensic Certified Public

Accountant, and Forensic Certified Public Accountant, am still looking for a great wife. I may have to get

some help from Santa Claus. There is no one better to ask for help in finding a pretty and nice female

that will become my wife. Since, I am looking for a great female wife. Why not ask for a precious gift at

Christmastime. That is one of my dreams. Maybe, it will come true this year because that would be

very nice.

   As Treasurer of the "Santa Claus Trust Fund Account Number 1225", I, Titus Uno, Certified Public

Accountant, Forensic Certified Public Accountant, and Chartered Global Management Accountant, have

to make sure that this Sub-Account: the Christmas Ice-Skating Sub-Account Number 1225.12, is

magically perfect and accurately accountable for the trustees of the "Santa Claus Trust Fund Account

Number 1225."

   The Christmas Ice-Skating Sub-Account Number 1225.12 of the "Santa Claus Trust Fund Account

Number 1225" has to be approved by the Treasurer which happens to be me, Titus Uno, Certified Public

Accountant, Forensic Certified Public Accountant, and Chartered Global Management Accountant. The

factor of naughty or nice is what has to be evaluated in order for the "Santa Claus Trust Fund Account

Number 1225" to be able to continue to be useful to continue the Christmas Ice-Skating Sub-Account

Number 1225.12. I, Titus Uno, Certified Public Accountant, Forensic Certified Public Accountant, and

Chartered Global Management Accountant, get to work with Santa Claus, Mrs. Santa Claus, and the

Head Elf that is under Mr. and Mrs. Santa Claus, and the Accountant Elf. Every Santa Claus that helps

with the Christmas Ice-Skating Sub-Account Number 1225.12 is evaluated to make sure that nice is

accurately entered beside every Santa Claus that helps with the Christmas Ice-Skating Sub-Account

Number 1225.12. If naughty is entered beside even just one Santa Claus that helps with the Christmas

Ice-Skating Sub-Account Number 1225.12, then there is a problem. However, there has never been a naughty enter by any Santa Claus that helps with the Christmas Ice-Skating Sub-Account Number 1225.12. There is a very low possibility that naughty will ever be placed by a Santa Claus that helps with the Christmas Ice-Skating Sub-Account Number 1225.12. I, Titus Uno, Certified Public Accountant, Forensic Certified Public Accountant, and Chartered Global Management Accountant, have to make sure that the naughty is changed to nice so that the Christmas Ice-Skating Sub-Account Number 1225.12 of the "Santa Claus Trust Fund Account Number 1225" can continue to be used for nice and not naughty or for good and not bad.

Santa Claus started a Christmas Ice-Skating Sub-Account Number 1225.12 as a part of the "Santa Claus Trust Fund Account Number 1225."

Chapter 14 the Christmas Parade with Santa Claus

The Christmas Parade with Santa Claus Sub-Account Number 1225.13 is a Sub-Account of the "Santa Claus Trust Fund Account Number 1225."

The purpose of the Christmas Parade with Santa Claus Sub-Account Number 1225.13 is to allow the Christmas Parade with Santa Claus Sub-Account to enable the Christmas Season to be as magical as it can by using the monies from this fund. These monies allow the Christmas Parade with Santa Claus Sub-Account to be more effective because more training can be made available to all of the Santa Clauses to allow the Christmas Parade with Santa Claus to be great. All of these Santa Clauses are prepared for any situation that can possibly happen with the Christmas Parade with Santa Claus. The Christmas Parade with Santa Claus is always exciting to be at or to watch on the television.

The Christmas Parade is an awesome family activity that families do together at Christmas. Santa Claus is always at the end of the Christmas Parade. He always waves at the children. Every child is excited to see Santa Claus. That is the perfect ending for every Christmas Parade. The Christmas Parade with Santa Claus Sub-Account Number 1225.13 is a Sub-Account of the "Santa Claus Trust Fund Account Number 1225" that assist in the presentation of all of the Christmas Parades this are presented in all of the cities all over the world. Of course, every Christmas Parade has different amount of funds that are available for their Christmas Parade. These monies are almost doubled because of the Santa Claus Sub-Account Number 1225.13 is a Sub-Account of the "Santa Claus Trust Fund Account Number 1225." This increase allows for more floats, bands, and more entries to be able for the Christmas Parade in every city all over the world.

As Treasurer of the "Santa Claus Trust Fund Account Number 1225", I, Titus Uno, Certified Public Accountant, Forensic Certified Public Accountant, and Chartered Global Management Accountant, have to make sure that this Sub-Account: the Christmas Parade with Santa Claus Sub-Account Number 1225.13, is magically perfect and accurately accountable for the trustees of the "Santa Claus Trust Fund Account Number 1225."

The Christmas Parade with Santa Claus Sub-Account Number 1225.13 of the "Santa Claus Trust Fund Account Number 1225" has to be approved by the Treasurer which happens to be me, Titus Uno, Certified Public Accountant, Forensic Certified Public Accountant, and Chartered Global Management Accountant. The factor of naughty or nice is what has to be evaluated in order for the "Santa Claus Trust Fund Account Number 1225" to be able to continue to be useful to continue the Christmas Parade with Santa Claus Sub-Account Number 1225.13. I, Titus Uno, Certified Public Accountant, Forensic Certified Public Accountant, and Chartered Global Management Accountant, get to work with Santa Claus, Mrs. Santa Claus, and the Head Elf that is under Mr. and Mrs. Santa Claus, and the Accountant Elf. Every Santa Claus that helps with the Christmas Parade with Santa Claus Sub-Account Number 1225.13 is evaluated to make sure that nice is accurately entered beside every Santa Claus that helps with the Christmas Parade with Santa Claus Sub-Account Number 1225.13. If naughty is entered beside even just one Santa Claus that helps with the Christmas Parade with Santa Claus Sub-Account Number 1225.13, then there is a problem. However, there has never been a naughty enter by any Santa Claus that helps with the Christmas Parade with Santa Claus Sub-Account Number 1225.13. There is a very low possibility that naughty will ever be placed by a Santa Claus that helps with the Christmas Parade with Santa Claus Sub-Account Number 1225.13. I, Titus Uno, Certified Public Accountant, Forensic Certified Public Accountant, and Chartered Global Management Accountant, have to make sure that the naughty is changed to nice so that the Christmas Parade with Santa Claus Sub-Account Number 1225.13 of the

"Santa Claus Trust Fund Account Number 1225" can continue to be used for good and not bad or for nice and not naughty.

Santa Claus started a Christmas Parade with Santa Claus Sub-Account Number 1225.13 as a part of the "Santa Claus Trust Fund Account Number 1225."

Chapter 15 the Christmas Presents

The Christmas Presents Sub-Account Number 1225.14 is a Sub-Account of the "Santa Claus Trust Fund Account Number 1225."

The purpose of the Christmas Presents Sub-Account Number 1225.14 is to allow the Christmas Presents Sub-Account to enable the Christmas Season to be as magical as it can by using the monies from this fund. These monies allow the Christmas Presents Sub-Account to be more effective because more training can be made available to all of the Santa Clauses to give Christmas Presents. All of these Santa Clauses are prepared for any situation that can possibly happen in delivering and presenting the Christmas Presents to the children.

Gifts are exciting to receive and to give. Both the gift giver and the gift recipient benefit from the giving of the Christmas Presents.

Giving gifts is a part of Christmas time. It is not nice to not think of others at Christmastime. It is so exciting to make other people feel great during the Christmas Season. The Christmas Spirit is also included in giving Christmas Gifts or Presents because giving gifts helps the gift recipient to feel like helping other people. This causes more and more people to have the Christmas Spirit.

Receiving gifts is also a part of Christmas time. If someone somehow does not receive a Christmas Present that would not be nice. Everyone in the whole world should receive at least one Christmas Present every Christmas. The Christmas Presents Sub-Account Number 1225.14 is a Sub-Account of the "Santa Claus Trust Fund Account Number 1225" helps to make sure that everyone in the whole world receives at least one Christmas Present every Christmas. This makes sure that someone who does not receive a Christmas Present will not turn into a naughty or not nice person the whole year.

As Treasurer of the "Santa Claus Trust Fund Account Number 1225", I, Titus Uno, Certified Public Accountant, Forensic Certified Public Accountant, and Chartered Global Management Accountant, have to make sure that this Sub-Account: the Christmas Presents Sub-Account Number 1225.14, is magically perfect and accurately accountable for the trustees of the "Santa Claus Trust Fund Account Number 1225."

The Christmas Presents Sub-Account Number 1225.14 of the "Santa Claus Trust Fund Account Number 1225" has to be approved by the Treasurer which happens to be me, Titus Uno, Certified Public Accountant, Forensic Certified Public Accountant, and Chartered Global Management Accountant. The factor of naughty or nice is what has to be evaluated in order for the "Santa Claus Trust Fund Account Number 1225" to be able to continue to be useful to continue the Christmas Presents Sub-Account Number 1225.14. I, Titus Uno, Certified Public Accountant, Forensic Certified Public Accountant, and Chartered Global Management Accountant, get to work with Santa Claus, Mrs. Santa Claus, and the Head Elf that is under Mr. and Mrs. Santa Claus, and the Accountant Elf. Every Santa Claus that helps with the Christmas Presents Sub-Account Number 1225.14 is evaluated to make sure that nice is accurately entered beside every Santa Claus that helps with the Christmas Presents Sub-Account Number 1225.14. If naughty is entered beside even just one Santa Claus that helps with the Christmas Presents Sub-Account Number 1225.14, then there is a problem. However, there has never been a naughty enter by any Santa Claus that helps with the Christmas Presents Sub-Account Number 1225.14. There is a very low possibility that naughty will ever be placed by a Santa Claus that helps with the Christmas Presents Sub-Account Number 1225.14. I, Titus Uno, Certified Public Accountant, Forensic Certified Public Accountant, and Chartered Global Management Accountant, have to make sure that the naughty is changed to nice so that the Christmas Presents Sub-Account Number 1225.14 of the "Santa Claus Trust Fund Account Number 1225" can continue to be used for nice and not naughty or for good and not bad.

Santa Claus started a Christmas Presents Sub-Account Number 1225.14 as a part of the "Santa Claus Trust Fund Account Number 1225."

The Christmas Trees Sub-Account Number 1225.15 is a Sub-Account of the "Santa Claus Trust Fund Account Number 1225."

The purpose of the Christmas Trees Sub-Account Number 1225.15 is to allow the Christmas Trees Sub-Account to enable the Christmas Season to be as magical as it can by using the monies from this fund. These monies allow the Christmas Trees Sub-Account to be more effective because more training can be made available to all of the Santa Clauses help people be prepared by having their Christmas Trees. All of these Santa Clauses are prepared for any situation that can possibly happen in the preparations of their Christmas Trees.

The Family Christmas Tree is very important to every family that celebrates Christmas. It is very fun to decorate the Family Christmas Tree every Christmas as a family Christmas event.

The Christmas Tree Farms are a great place to find the perfect Christmas Trees for all the families to place in their houses that will be decorated. These Christmas Tree Farms are where professional Christmas Trees are grown just for this purpose.

The City Christmas Trees are very large Christmas Trees that the city decorates for all of the locals and visitors can enjoy as they pass by the City Christmas Trees that are beautifully decorated by the city.

The National Christmas Trees are Christmas Trees that are decorated by the United States of America Government. These trees are located at the National Landmarks for tourists to enjoy as these National Landmarks are being visited by locals and by visitors.

Christmas Trees are everywhere during Christmastime. The Christmas Trees Sub-Account Number 1225.15 is a Sub-Account of the "Santa Claus Trust Fund Account Number 1225" helps in the decorating of every Christmas tree that is decorated during Christmastime.

As Treasurer of the "Santa Claus Trust Fund Account Number 1225", I, Titus Uno, Certified Public Accountant, Forensic Certified Public Accountant, and Chartered Global Management Accountant, have to make sure that this Sub-Account: the Christmas Trees Sub-Account Number 1225.15, is magically perfect and accurately accountable for the trustees of the "Santa Claus Trust Fund Account Number 1225."

The Christmas Trees Sub-Account Number 1225.15 of the "Santa Claus Trust Fund Account Number 1225" has to be approved by the Treasurer which happens to be me, Titus Uno, Certified Public Accountant, Forensic Certified Public Accountant, and Chartered Global Management Accountant. The factor of naughty or nice is what has to be evaluated in order for the "Santa Claus Trust Fund Account Number 1225" to be able to continue to be useful to continue the Christmas Trees Sub-Account Number 1225.15. I, Titus Uno, Certified Public Accountant, Forensic Certified Public Accountant, and Chartered Global Management Accountant, get to work with Santa Claus, Mrs. Santa Claus, and the Head Elf that is under Mr. and Mrs. Santa Claus, and the Accountant Elf. Every Santa Claus that helps with the Christmas Trees Sub-Account Number 1225.15 is evaluated to make sure that nice is accurately entered beside every Santa Claus that helps with the Christmas Trees Sub-Account Number 1225.15. If naughty is entered beside even just one Santa Claus that helps with the Christmas Trees Sub-Account Number 1225.15, then there is a problem. However, there has never been a naughty enter by any Santa Claus that helps with the Christmas Trees Sub-Account Number 1225.15. There is a very low possibility that naughty will ever be placed by a Santa Claus that helps with the Christmas Trees Sub-Account Number 1225.15. I, Titus Uno, Certified Public Accountant, Forensic Certified Public Accountant, and Chartered Global Management Accountant, have to make sure that the naughty is changed to nice so that the

Christmas Trees Sub-Account Number 1225.15 of the "Santa Claus Trust Fund Account Number 1225" can continue to be used for good and not bad or for nice and not naughty.

Santa Claus started a Christmas Trees Sub-Account Number 1225.15 as a part of the "Santa Claus Trust Fund Account Number 1225."

Chapter 17 the Christmas Parties

The Christmas Parties Sub-Account Number 1225.16 is a Sub-Account of the "Santa Claus Trust Fund Account Number 1225."

The purpose of the Christmas Parties Sub-Account Number 1225.16 is to allow the Christmas Parties Sub-Account to enable the Christmas Season to be as magical as it can by using the monies from this fund. These monies allow the Christmas Parties Sub-Account to be more effective because more training can be made available to all of the Santa Clauses to be present at Christmas Parties. All of these Santa Clauses are prepared for any situation that can possibly happen at a Christmas Party.

The Family Christmas Parties are exciting because all of the family members and all of the family member's friends are present at the Family Christmas Parties. It is great that every family member gets along with all of the other family members during Christmastime.

The Company Christmas Parties are attended by all of the company employees and their spouses.

The Church Christmas Parties are attended by the church members. These parties involve studying the bible and has a religious theme. Eating food and discussing the bible are activities of these parties. It is awesome to party with other religious people from your church and probably your Sunday School Class.

The Friends Christmas Parties are the parties that are attended by friends. These Friends Christmas Parties are very fun because all of the friends of the host of the Friends Christmas Party are present. These parties can include games (both box and video, dancing, watching movies, watching television shows, scavenger hunts, and preparing food and eating the food. I, Titus Uno, Certified Public Accountant, Forensic Certified Public Accountant, and Chartered Global Management Accountant, am over the Single Adult Ministries Class at my church. This is the best class because it is made up of Single people that are looking for nice activities to do with other nice single people that attend church. A church that is not interest in Single Adults is missing out on a great type of Christians. I, Titus Uno, Certified Public Accountant, Forensic Certified Public Accountant, and Chartered Global Management Accountant, am glad that my church really cares about Single Adults. This Sunday school gets together for Sunday school and at least one activity each week. The best activity is the Church Single Adult Christmas Party. All of the Church Single Adults bring a gift for our church program for a single parent that needs help with the purchase of a gift for that child. These presents are wrapped by all of the Church Single Adults that are at this party. Every year the participation in this activity has increased. In other words, it takes longer to wrap up all of these special gifts. It is great to help other people that needs help during Christmastime.

All of these Christmas Party types are important to get people in the Christmas Spirit by allowing the Christmas Party goers to interact with others and to not sit at home all by themselves. The Christmas Parties Sub-Account Number 1225.16 is a Sub-Account of the "Santa Claus Trust Fund Account Number 1225" allows these Christmas Parties to help all of the attendees to increase their Christmas Spirit at Christmastime.

As Treasurer of the "Santa Claus Trust Fund Account Number 1225", I, Titus Uno, Certified Public Accountant, Forensic Certified Public Accountant, and Chartered Global Management Accountant, have to make sure that this Sub-Account: the Christmas Parties Sub-Account Number 1225.16, is magically perfect and accurately accountable for the trustees of the "Santa Claus Trust Fund Account Number 1225."

The Christmas Parties Sub-Account Number 1225.16 of the "Santa Claus Trust Fund Account Number 1225" has to be approved by the Treasurer which happens to be me, Titus Uno, Certified Public

Accountant, Forensic Certified Public Accountant, and Chartered Global Management Accountant. The factor of naughty or nice is what has to be evaluated in order for the "Santa Claus Trust Fund Account Number 1225" to be able to continue to be useful to continue the Christmas Parties Sub-Account Number 1225.16. I, Titus Uno, Certified Public Accountant, Forensic Certified Public Accountant, and Chartered Global Management Accountant, get to work with Santa Claus, Mrs. Santa Claus, and the Head Elf that is under Mr. and Mrs. Santa Claus, and the Accountant Elf. Every Santa Claus that helps with the Christmas Parties Sub-Account Number 1225.16 is evaluated to make sure that nice is accurately entered beside every Santa Claus that helps with the Christmas Parties Sub-Account Number 1225.16. If naughty is entered beside even just one Santa Claus that helps with the Christmas Parties Sub-Account Number 1225.16, then there is a problem. However, there has never been a naughty enter by any Santa Claus that helps with the Christmas Parties Sub-Account Number 1225.16. There is a very low possibility that naughty will ever be placed by a Santa Claus that helps with the Christmas Parties Sub-Account Number 1225.16. I, Titus Uno, Certified Public Accountant, Forensic Certified Public Accountant, and Chartered Global Management Accountant, have to make sure that the naughty is changed to nice so that the Christmas Parties Sub-Account Number 1225.16 of the "Santa Claus Trust Fund Account Number 1225" can continue to be used for nice and not naughty or for good and not bad.

Santa Claus started a Christmas Parties Sub-Account Number 1225.16 as a part of the "Santa Claus Trust Fund Account Number 1225."

Chapter 18 the Christmas Carolers

The Christmas Carolers Sub-Account Number 1225.17 is a Sub-Account of the "Santa Claus Trust Fund Account Number 1225."

The purpose of the Christmas Carolers Sub-Account Number 1225.17 is to allow the Christmas Carolers Sub-Account to enable the Christmas Season to be as magical as it can by using the monies from this fund. These monies allow the Christmas Carolers Sub-Account to be more effective because more training can be made available to all of the Santa Clauses to sing along with Christmas Carolers. All of these Santa Clauses are prepared for any situation that can possibly happen in singing with the singing Christmas Carolers.

The Christmas Carolers singing is often present during Christmastime. It is awesome to play a horn or to sing a Christmas Carol to people at Christmastime. I, Titus Uno, Certified Public Accountant, Forensic Certified Public Accountant, and Chartered Global Management Accountant, have done both. I was so satisfied by participating in the Christmas Caroling at Christmastime.

Christmas Carolers sing songs to people in order to allow those people to increase their Christmas Spirit and to hopefully spread their Christmas Spirit to others. Christmas music is so uplifting to anyone that is able to hear this Christmas music. The Christmas Carolers Sub-Account Number 1225.17 is a Sub-Account of the "Santa Claus Trust Fund Account Number 1225" allows those Christmas Carolers to have more opportunities to sing their Christmas Carols to a greater number of listeners. This allows for more and more people to gain more and more Christmas Spirit during the Christmas Season. These Christmas Carols are very nice to hear. It is also fun to see and hear all of these songs that have been memorized by the singers.

As Treasurer of the "Santa Claus Trust Fund Account Number 1225", I, Titus Uno, Certified Public Accountant, Forensic Certified Public Accountant, and Chartered Global Management Accountant, have to make sure that this Sub-Account: the Christmas Carolers Sub-Account Number 1225.17, is magically perfect and accurately accountable for the trustees of the "Santa Claus Trust Fund Account Number 1225."

The Christmas Carolers Sub-Account Number 1225.17 of the "Santa Claus Trust Fund Account Number 1225" has to be approved by the Treasurer which happens to be me, Titus Uno, Certified Public Accountant, Forensic Certified Public Accountant, and Chartered Global Management Accountant. The factor of naughty or nice is what has to be evaluated in order for the "Santa Claus Trust Fund Account Number 1225" to be able to continue to be useful to continue the Christmas Carolers Sub-Account Number 1225.17. I, Titus Uno, Certified Public Accountant, Forensic Certified Public Accountant, and Chartered Global Management Accountant, get to work with Santa Claus, Mrs. Santa Claus, and the Head Elf that is under Mr. and Mrs. Santa Claus, and the Accountant Elf. Every Santa Claus that helps with the Christmas Carolers Sub-Account Number 1225.17 is evaluated to make sure that nice is accurately entered beside every Santa Claus that helps with the Christmas Carolers Sub-Account Number 1225.17. If naughty is entered beside even just one Santa Claus that helps with the Christmas Carolers Sub-Account Number 1225.17, then there is a problem. However, there has never been a naughty enter by any Santa Claus that helps with the Christmas Carolers Sub-Account Number 1225.17. There is a very low possibility that naughty will ever be placed by a Santa Claus that helps with the Christmas Carolers Sub-Account Number 1225.17. I , Titus Uno, Certified Public Accountant, Forensic Certified Public Accountant, and Chartered Global Management Accountant, have to make sure that the naughty is changed to nice s Christmas Carolers Sub-Account Number 1225.17 of the "Santa Claus Trust Fund Account Number 1225" can continue to be used for good and not bad or for nice and not naughty.

Santa Claus started a Christmas Carolers Sub-Account Number 1225.17 as a part of the "Santa Claus Trust Fund Account Number 1225."

Chapter 19 the Christmas Church Bells

The Christmas Church Bells Sub-Account Number 1225.18 is a Sub-Account of the "Santa Claus Trust Fund Account Number 1225."

The purpose of the Christmas Church Bells Sub-Account Number 1225.18 is to allow the Christmas Church Bells Sub-Account to enable the Christmas Season to be as magical as it can by using the monies from this fund. These monies allow the Christmas Church Bells Sub-Account to be more effective because more training can be made available to all of the Santa Clauses to help people go to Church when they hear the Christmas Church Bells ring. All of these Santa Clauses are prepared for any situation that can possibly happen when the Christmas Church Bells ring.

The Church Bells ring to tell people that it is Christmastime. Some churches have actual Church Bells that informs the people that are going to church that it is time to attend the Christmas Church Service. The Church Bells play pretty melodies for their songs.

The Christmas Church Hand Bells are a part of the Church Music Program. The Christmas Church Hand Bells are so exciting to hear and also are exciting to play. I, Titus Uno, Certified Public Accountant, Forensic Certified Public Accountant, Chartered Global Management Accountant, have also played in my Church's Hand Bell as a Bass Hand Bell Player. It is exciting being a musical Certified Public Accountant, Forensic Certified Public Accountant, and Chartered Global Management Accountant.

The Christmas Church Bells signal that it is time for the busiest day of churches because the pews are filled with every family member and their friends. Christmas and Easter are the best congregation numbers for most churches. The Christmas Church Bells Sub-Account Number 1225.18 is a Sub-Account of the "Santa Claus Trust Fund Account Number 1225" helps to restore all of the Church Bells that did not work or helps to get more Churches to ring their Church Bells for their Christmas Church Service by the regular church members and for the church visitors.

As Treasurer of the "Santa Claus Trust Fund Account Number 1225", I, Titus Uno, Certified Public Accountant, Forensic Certified Public Accountant, and Chartered Global Management Accountant, have to make sure that this Sub-Account: the Christmas Church Bells Sub-Account Number 1225.18, is magically perfect and accurately accountable for the trustees of the "Santa Claus Trust Fund Account Number 1225."

The Christmas Church Bells Sub-Account Number 1225.18 of the "Santa Claus Trust Fund Account Number 1225" has to be approved by the Treasurer which happens to be me, Titus Uno, Certified Public Accountant, Forensic Certified Public Accountant, and Chartered Global Management Accountant. The factor of naughty or nice is what has to be evaluated in order for the "Santa Claus Trust Fund Account Number 1225" to be able to continue to be useful to continue the Christmas Church Bells Sub-Account Number 1225.18. I, Titus Uno, Certified Public Accountant, Forensic Certified Public Accountant, and Chartered Global Management Accountant, get to work with Santa Claus, Mrs. Santa Claus, and the Head Elf that is under Mr. and Mrs. Santa Claus, and the Accountant Elf. Every Santa Claus that helps with the Christmas Church Bells Sub-Account Number 1225.18 is evaluated to make sure that nice is accurately entered beside every Santa Claus that helps with the Christmas Church Bells Sub-Account Number 1225.18. If naughty is entered beside even just one Santa Claus that helps with the Christmas Church Bells Sub-Account Number 1225.18, then there is a problem. However, there has never been a naughty enter by any Santa Claus that helps with the Christmas Church Bells Sub-Account Number 1225.18. There is a very low possibility that naughty will ever be placed by a Santa Claus that helps with the Christmas Church Bells Sub-Account Number 1225.18. I , Titus Uno, Certified Public Accountant, Forensic Certified Public Accountant, and Chartered Global Management Accountant, have to make sure that the naughty is changed to nice so that the Christmas Church Bells Sub-Account Number 1225.18 of the "Santa Claus Trust Fund Account Number 1225" can continue to be used for nice and not naughty or for good and not bad.

Santa Claus started a Christmas Church Bells Sub-Account Number 1225.18 as a part of the "Santa Claus Trust Fund Account Number 1225."

The Christmas Mistletoe and the Magical Kiss Sub-Account Number 1225.19 is a Sub-Account of the "Santa Claus Trust Fund Account Number 1225."

The purpose of the Christmas Mistletoe and the Magical Kiss Sub-Account Number 1225.19 is to allow the Christmas Mistletoe and the Magical Kiss Sub-Account to enable the Christmas Season to be as magical as it can by using the monies from this fund. These monies allow the Christmas Mistletoe and the Magical Kiss Sub-Account to be more effective because more training can be made available to all of the Santa Clauses to assist in the placement of the Christmas Mistletoe and the Magical Kiss. All of these Santa Clauses are prepared for any situation that can possibly happen in the placement of the Christmas Mistletoe so the Magical Kiss will occur. The Christmas Mistletoe and the Magical Kiss Sub-Account Number 1225.19 is a Sub-Account of the "Santa Claus Trust Fund Account Number 1225" helps to assist in the placement of the Christmas Mistletoe in perfect strategic location for maximum kissing by single people that will lead to marriage because of these kisses under the Christmas Mistletoe.

Christmas Mistletoe under a doorway. Many couples have been married because of the Christmas Mistletoe under a doorway. The doorway is a great surprise for these single people that are looking to get married. Some single people need a little help kissing each other. The Christmas Mistletoe is a great reason to kiss because it is the custom for single people to kiss if they are underneath the Christmas Mistletoe.

The Christmas Mistletoe can be placed over a swing. This is another great place to cause these single people or couple to kiss underneath the Christmas Mistletoe. The Christmas Mistletoe should be small enough to be hidden from the two single people, but large enough to be found eventually by the two single people so that they will kiss. This kiss might lead this single pair of singles to end with marriage to each other.

As Treasurer of the "Santa Claus Trust Fund Account Number 1225", I, Titus Uno, Certified Public Accountant, Forensic Certified Public Accountant, and Chartered Global Management Accountant, have to make sure that this Sub-Account: the Christmas Mistletoe and the Magical Kiss Sub-Account Number 1225.19, is magically perfect and accurately accountable for the trustees of the "Santa Claus Trust Fund Account Number 1225."

The Christmas Mistletoe and the Magical Kiss Sub-Account Number 1225.19 of the "Santa Claus Trust Fund Account Number 1225" has to be approved by the Treasurer which happens to be me, Titus Uno, Certified Public Accountant, Forensic Certified Public Accountant, and Chartered Global Management Accountant. The factor of naughty or nice is what has to be evaluated in order for the "Santa Claus Trust Fund Account Number 1225" to be able to continue to be useful to continue the Christmas Mistletoe and the Magical Kiss Sub-Account Number 1225.19. I, Titus Uno, Certified Public Accountant, Forensic Certified Public Accountant, and Chartered Global Management Accountant, get to work with Santa Claus, Mrs. Santa Claus, and the Head Elf that is under Mr. and Mrs. Santa Claus, and the Accountant Elf. Every Santa Claus that helps with the Christmas Mistletoe and the Magical Kiss Sub-Account Number 1225.19 is evaluated to make sure that nice is accurately entered beside every Santa Claus that helps with the Christmas Mistletoe and the Magical Kiss Sub-Account Number 1225.19. If naughty is entered beside even just one Santa Claus that helps with the Christmas Mistletoe and the Magical Kiss Sub-Account Number 1225.19, then there is a problem. However, there has never been a naughty enter by any Santa Claus that helps with the Christmas Mistletoe and the Magical Kiss Sub-Account Number 1225.19. There is a very low possibility that naughty will ever be placed by a Santa Claus that helps with the Christmas Mistletoe and the Magical Kiss Sub-Account Number 1225.19. I, Titus Uno, Certified Public Accountant, Forensic Certified Public Accountant, and Chartered Global Management

Accountant, have to make sure that the naughty is changed to nice so that the Christmas Mistletoe and the Magical Kiss Sub-Account Number 1225.19 of the "Santa Claus Trust Fund Account Number 1225" can continue to be used for good and not bad or for nice and not naughty.

Santa Claus started a Christmas Mistletoe and the Magical Kiss Sub-Account Number 1225.19 as a part of the "Santa Claus Trust Fund Account Number 1225."

Chapter 21 the Christmas Snowman

The Christmas Snowman Sub-Account Number 1225.20 is a Sub-Account of the "Santa Claus Trust Fund Account Number 1225."

The purpose of the Christmas Snowman Sub-Account Number 1225.20 is to allow the Christmas Snowman Sub-Account to enable the Christmas Season to be as magical as it can by using the monies from this fund. These monies allow the Christmas Snowman Sub-Account to be more effective because more training can be made available to all of the Santa Clauses can assist in the building of the Christmas Snowman. All of these Santa Clauses are prepared for any situation that can possibly happen in the building of the Christmas Snowman.

The Christmas Snowman is another great family activity for families that live where it snows enough for the families to build a snowman. The building of snowmen are fun to build and to decorate by every member of the family. The body and head of the Christmas Snowman are rolled. The head is decorated to form the eyes and nose. A hat is placed on the top of the head. A scarf is placed around the neck of the Christmas Snowman. Large sticks form the arms of the Christmas Snowman. The Christmas Snowman Sub-Account Number 1225.20 is a Sub-Account of the "Santa Claus Trust Fund Account Number 1225" assists families in the building of Christmas Snowman on every neighborhood house to show that families have Christmas Spirit. These Christmas Snowmen show that families work together to for the Christmas Snowman.

Some Christmas Snowmen are large and some Christmas Snowmen are small, but each Christmas Snowman is very special. Every family worked hard together to build each and every Christmas Snowman.

As Treasurer of the "Santa Claus Trust Fund Account Number 1225", I, Titus Uno, Certified Public Accountant, Forensic Certified Public Accountant, and Chartered Global Management Accountant, have to make sure that this Sub-Account: the Christmas Snowman Sub-Account Number 1225.20 is magically perfect and accurately accountable for the trustees of the "Santa Claus Trust Fund Account Number 1225."

The Christmas Snowman Sub-Account Number 1225.20 of the "Santa Claus Trust Fund Account Number 1225" has to be approved by the Treasurer which happens to be me, Titus Uno, Certified Public Accountant, Forensic Certified Public Accountant, and Chartered Global Management Accountant. The factor of naughty or nice is what has to be evaluated in order for the "Santa Claus Trust Fund Account Number 1225" to be able to continue to be useful to continue the Christmas Snowman Sub-Account Number 1225.20. I, Titus Uno, Certified Public Accountant, Forensic Certified Public Accountant, and Chartered Global Management Accountant, get to work with Santa Claus, Mrs. Santa Claus, and the Head Elf that is under Mr. and Mrs. Santa Claus, and the Accountant Elf. Every Santa Claus that helps with the Christmas Snowman Sub-Account Number 1225.20 is evaluated to make sure that nice is accurately entered beside every Santa Claus that helps with the Christmas Snowman Sub-Account Number 1225.20. If naughty is entered beside even just one Santa Claus that helps with the Christmas Snowman Sub-Account Number 1225.20, then there is a problem. However, there has never been a naughty enter by any Santa Claus that helps with the Christmas Snowman Sub-Account Number 1225.20. There is a very low possibility that naughty will ever be placed by a Santa Claus that helps with the Christmas Snowman Sub-Account Number 1225.20. I , Titus Uno, Certified Public Accountant, Forensic Certified Public Accountant, and Chartered Global Management Accountant, have to make sure that the naughty is changed to nice so that the Christmas Snowman Sub-Account Number 1225.20 of the "Santa Claus Trust Fund Account Number 1225" can continue to be used for nice and not naughty or for good and not bad.

Santa Claus started a Christmas Snowman Sub-Account Number 1225.20 as a part of the "Santa Claus Trust Fund Account Number 1225."

Chapter 22 the Christmas Mall Santa Claus and the Picture with that Christmas Mall Santa Claus

The Christmas Mall Santa Claus and the Picture with that Christmas Mall Santa Claus Sub-Account Number 1225.21 is a Sub-Account of the "Santa Claus Trust Fund Account Number 1225."

The purpose of the Christmas Mall Santa Claus and the Picture with that Christmas Mall Santa Claus Sub-Account Number 1225.21 is to allow the Christmas Mall Santa Claus and the Picture with that Christmas Mall Santa Claus Sub-Account to enable the Christmas Season to be as magical as it can by using the monies from this fund. These monies allow the Christmas Mall Santa Claus and the Picture with that Christmas Mall Santa Claus Santa Claus and the Picture with that Christmas Mall Santa Claus to be more effective because more training can be made available to all of the Santa Clauses in the taking of the Picture with that Christmas Mall Santa Claus. All of these Santa Clauses are prepared for any situation that can possibly happen in the taking of the Picture with that Christmas Mall Santa Claus.

Santa Claus has his picture taken with children, pets, and sometime with even adults. Santa Claus really loves everyone that believes in Santa Claus. Children, pets, and adults are all loved by Santa Claus, and the children, pets, and adults love Santa Claus. It is so awesome how this interaction goes so smoothly. Of course, there are those rare moments that are sometimes captured by the camera, but for the most part everything is going great. The main purpose of this picture taking is to capture the meeting of Santa Claus and to tell Santa Claus what is wanted.

As Treasurer of the "Santa Claus Trust Fund Account Number 1225", I, Titus Uno, Certified Public Accountant, Forensic Certified Public Accountant, and Chartered Global Management Accountant, have to make sure that this Sub-Account: the Christmas Mall Santa Claus and the Picture with that Christmas

Mall Santa Claus Sub-Account Number 1225.21 is magically perfect and accurately accountable for the trustees of the "Santa Claus Trust Fund Account Number 1225."

The Christmas Mall Santa Claus and the Picture with that Christmas Mall Santa Claus Sub-Account Number 1225.21 of the "Santa Claus Trust Fund Account Number 1225" has to be approved by the Treasurer which happens to be me, Titus Uno, Certified Public Accountant, Forensic Certified Public Accountant, and Chartered Global Management Accountant. The factor of naughty or nice is what has to be evaluated in order for the "Santa Claus Trust Fund Account Number 1225" to be able to continue to be useful to continue the Christmas Mall Santa Claus and the Picture with that Christmas Mall Santa Claus Sub-Account Number 1225.2. I, Titus Uno, Certified Public Accountant, Forensic Certified Public Accountant, and Chartered Global Management Accountant, get to work with Santa Claus, Mrs. Santa Claus, and the Head Elf that is under Mr. and Mrs. Santa Claus, and the Accountant Elf. Every Santa Claus that helps with the Christmas Mall Santa Claus and the Picture with that Christmas Mall Santa Claus Sub-Account Number 1225.21 is evaluated to make sure that nice is accurately entered beside every Santa Claus that helps with the Christmas Mall Santa Claus and the Picture with that Christmas Mall Santa Claus Sub-Account Number 1225.21. If naughty is entered beside even just one Santa Claus that helps with the Christmas Mall Santa Claus and the Picture with that Christmas Mall Santa Claus Sub-Account Number 1225.21, then there is a problem. However, there has never been a naughty enter by any Santa Claus that helps with the Christmas Mall Santa Claus and the Picture with that Christmas Mall Santa Claus Sub-Account Number 1225.21. There is a very low possibility that naughty will ever be placed by a Santa Claus that helps with the Christmas Mall Santa Claus and the Picture with that Christmas Mall Santa Claus Sub-Account Number 1225.21. I, Titus Uno, Certified Public Accountant, Forensic Certified Public Accountant, and Chartered Global Management Accountant, have to make sure that the naughty is changed to nice so that the Christmas Mall Santa Claus and the Picture with that

Christmas Mall Santa Claus Sub-Account Number 1225.21 of the "Santa Claus Trust Fund Account

Number 1225" can continue to be used for good and not bad or for nice and not naughty.

Santa Claus started a Christmas Mall Santa Claus and the Picture with that Christmas Mall Santa Claus

Sub-Account Number 1225.21 as a part of the "Santa Claus Trust Fund Account Number 1225."

Chapter 23 the Christmas Miracles

The Christmas Miracles Sub-Account Number 1225.22 is a Sub-Account of the "Santa Claus Trust Fund Account Number 1225." The Christmas Miracles happen all around us even if it is not Christmastime. These Christmas Miracles are what makes life bearable and worth living. It is so amazing when something happen out of the blue, and someone says that it is a miracle that this turned out this way.

The purpose of the Christmas Miracles Sub-Account Number 1225.22 is to allow the Christmas Miracles Sub-Account to enable the Christmas Season to be as magical as it can by using the monies from this fund. These monies allow the Christmas Miracles Sub-Account to be more effective because more training can be made available to all of the Santa Clauses to help Christmas Miracles occur. All of these Santa Clauses are prepared for any situation that can possibly happen to help Christmas Miracles occur.

Christmastime is the perfect time for miracles to happen. These Christmas Miracles are anything that happens that is not supposed to happen. Such as someone is expecting to get fired, but does not get fired. Another example would be someone owes money for their utility bills, but someone else takes care of the bills for that person. The Christmas Miracles Sub-Account Number 1225.22 is a Sub-Account of the "Santa Claus Trust Fund Account Number 1225" helps to assist in the performance of creating Christmas Miracles so that people's Christmas Spirit in increased. Christmas Miracles are a great way to make people feel great and have plenty of Christmas Spirit. Once someone has the Christmas Spirit, they want to spread that Christmas Spirit to other people. The more this Christmas Spirit spread the more it will spread. This is a very great occupancy at Christmastime.

As Treasurer of the "Santa Claus Trust Fund Account Number 1225", I, Titus Uno, Certified Public Accountant, Forensic Certified Public Accountant, and Chartered Global Management Accountant, have to make sure that this Sub-Account: the Christmas Miracles Sub-Account Number 1225.22 is magically perfect and accurately accountable for the trustees of the "Santa Claus Trust Fund Account Number 1225."

The Christmas Miracles Sub-Account Number 1225.22 of the "Santa Claus Trust Fund Account Number 1225" has to be approved by the Treasurer which happens to be me, Titus Uno, Certified Public Accountant, Forensic Certified Public Accountant, and Chartered Global Management Accountant. The factor of naughty or nice is what has to be evaluated in order for the "Santa Claus Trust Fund Account Number 1225" to be able to continue to be useful to continue the Christmas Miracles Sub-Account Number 1225.22. I, Titus Uno, Certified Public Accountant, Forensic Certified Public Accountant, and Chartered Global Management Accountant, get to work with Santa Claus, Mrs. Santa Claus, and the Head Elf that is under Mr. and Mrs. Santa Claus, and the Accountant Elf. Every Santa Claus that helps with the Christmas Miracles Sub-Account Number 1225.22 is evaluated to make sure that nice is accurately entered beside every Santa Claus that helps with the Christmas Miracles Sub-Account Number 1225.22. If naughty is entered beside even just one Santa Claus that helps with the Christmas Miracles Sub-Account Number 1225.22, then there is a problem. However, there has never been a naughty enter by any Santa Claus that helps with the Christmas Miracles Sub-Account Number 1225.22. There is a very low possibility that naughty will ever be placed by a Santa Claus that helps with the Christmas Miracles Sub-Account Number 1225.22. I, Titus Uno, Certified Public Accountant, Forensic Certified Public Accountant, and Chartered Global Management Accountant, have to make sure that the naughty is changed to nice so that the Christmas Miracles Sub-Account Number 1225.22 of the "Santa Claus Trust Fund Account Number 1225" can continue to be used for nice and not naughty or for good and not bad.

Santa Claus started a Christmas Miracles Sub-Account Number 1225.22 as a part of the "Santa Claus Trust Fund Account Number 1225."

Chapter 24 the Court Case of the "Santa Claus Trust Fund Account Number 1225" or the Christmas Donor

The Court Case will determine the future of the "Santa Claus Trust Fund Account Number 1225." The outcome that will be announced has to come out with a verdict of the "Santa Claus Trust Fund Account Number 1225" has to be allowed to continue.

Knott Nice threw a wrinkle into the smooth operations of the account called the "Santa Claus Trust Fund Account Number 1225." Knott Nice tried to use the "Santa Claus Trust Fund Account Number 1225" for Knott Nice's own good by not being nice or good. Knott Nice use the "Santa Claus Trust Fund Account Number 1225" to help people be mean.

There was this very nice person that was so friendly that Knott Nice got into the heart of this very nice person's bosses. These bosses basically told this very nice person to become as mean as these bosses or this very nice person would be let go. This made this very nice person sad. However, the choice was very easy to decide. This very nice person could not go against being nice.

These bosses did not stop there. These bosses spread rumors and made everyone laugh at this very nice person. Everyone would say that no one would ever want to marry this nice person. This made this very nice person very sad. No matter where this very nice person would go, he would hear laughter and mean things said about him. Such as "He will never get married" or "She does not need him."

This very nice person finally decided to sell everything and move away, so that he could do good wherever he decides to go. He traveled and traveled. This very nice person finally came to a place that was made entirely of nice people. These nice people made him feel right at home because everyone was nice.

This very nice person became so popular that he became mayor. As mayor, this very nice person decided to make this town a toy making town. This very nice person came up with the most amazing idea. He thought that it would be awesome to teach all of the children in the world that it is better to be nice instead of naughty like the very nice person's bosses were to the very nice person.

Time went by and this very nice man got older and he grew a mustache and beard. This very nice person loved wearing a red suit and hat. Big black boots made it easier get around in the snow that was outside. This very nice person gained popularity and in the United States of America, he became known as Santa Claus.

Knott Nice picked the wrong person to go against. Santa Claus was created thanks to Knott Nice making those bosses to be mean to Santa Claus.

Knott Nice lost the court case by Santa Claus staying true and moral. I guess it is true that it is better to be nice than to be Knott Nice. That is where this saying comes from. Knott Nice was rich because he was Knott Nice. The Christmas Court made Knott Nice set up an account called the "Santa Claus Trust Fund Account Number 1225" retroactive back to when Santa Claus came to exist. It is cool when magic is available. In other words, Knott Nice was trying to use his own money to be mean to Santa Claus before Santa Claus became Santa Claus.

Knott Nice helped Santa Claus to create the Nice or Knott Nice list. Over time it was changed to the Nice or Not Nice list. Most people now call it the Nice or Naughty List. Every child wants to be on the Nice list and not on the Knott Nice list. The ruling against Knott Nice really changed the fate of other people by the "Santa Claus Trust Fund Account Number 1225" being set up to help not nice people to become nice people.

Santa Claus has become a very important symbol of Christmas. Santa Claus does so much good promoting niceness and kindness that people all over the world are also nice. It only takes a few not nice people to mess everything up for nice people, but nice people stay nice no matter what happens. The not nice people are the people that need to change and become nice. Being nice makes people feel better than being "Knott" Nice.

So you had better be nice to others that you meet, instead of being "Knott" Nice to other people that you meet.

Chapter 25 the Conclusion by Titus Uno Certified Public Accountant, Forensic Certified Public Accountant, Chartered Global Management Accountant

The conclusion by Titus Uno, Certified Public Accountant, Forensic Certified Public Accountant, Chartered Global Management Accountant, is about how the "Santa Claus Trust Fund Account Number 1225" is continuing to be spent for the benefit of Christmas. The "Santa Claus Trust Fund Account Number 1225" is a very important and special account with 22 Sub-Accounts.

The Santa Claus Convention Sub-Account Number 1225.01, the Christmas Spirit Sub-Account Number 1225.02, the Christmas Secret Santa Sub-Account Number 1225.03, the Christmas Santa Letters Sub-Account Number 1225.04, the Santa Claus Bell Ringers for the Salvation Army Sub-Account Number 1225.05, the Christmas Eve Santa Claus Deliveries Sub-Account Number 1225.06, the Christmas Meals Sub-Account Number 1225.07, the Christmas Decorations Sub-Account0 Number 1225.08, the Christmas Candy Canes Sub-Account Number 1225.09, the Christmas Gingerbread House Sub-Account Number 1225.10, the Christmas Fruitcake Sub-Account Number 1225.11, the Christmas Ice-Skating Sub-Account Number 1225.12, the Christmas Parade with Santa Claus Sub-Account Number 1225.13, the Christmas Presents Sub-Account Number 1225.14, the Christmas Trees Sub-Account Number 1225.15, the Christmas Parties Sub-Account Number 1225.16, the Christmas Carolers Sub-Account Number 1225.17, the Christmas Church Bells Sub-Account Number 1225.18, the Christmas Mistletoe and the Magical Kiss Sub-Account Number 1225.19, the Christmas Snowman Sub-Account Number 1225.20, the Christmas Mall Santa Claus and the Picture with that Christmas Mall Santa Claus Sub-Account Number 1225.21, and the Christmas Miracles Sub-Account Number 1225.22 are all being accounted for with a purpose of making the "Santa Claus Trust Fund Account Number 1225" a very special Christmas be nice account as the Christmas donor directed.

The Santa Claus Convention Sub-Account Number 1225.01 will continue to operate as a nice Santa Claus Sub-Account to ensure that the Santa Claus Convention does promote the directives of the "Santa Claus Trust Fund Account Number 1225." All of the activities of the Santa Claus Convention Sub-Account Number 1225.01 are categorized as nice. None the activities of the Santa Claus Convention Sub-Account Number 1225.01 are categorized as naughty. That is the reason that the activities of the Santa Claus Convention Sub-Account Number 1225.01 will continue to operate as directed by the "Santa Claus Trust Fund Account Number 1225." Thank you Greenland and Poland for hosting this Year's Santa Claus Convention. That was very nice.

The Christmas Spirit Sub-Account Number 1225.02 will continue to operate as a nice Santa Claus Sub-Account to ensure that the Christmas Spirit does promote the directives of the "Santa Claus Trust Fund Account Number 1225." All of the activities of the Christmas Spirit Sub-Account Number 1225.02 are categorized as nice. None the activities of the Christmas Spirit Sub-Account Number 1225.02 are categorized as naughty. That is the reason that the activities of the Christmas Spirit Sub-Account Number 1225.02 will continue to operate as directed by the "Santa Claus Trust Fund Account Number 1225."

The Christmas Secret Santa Sub-Account Number 1225.03 will continue to operate as a nice Santa Claus Sub-Account to ensure that the Christmas Secret Santa does promote the directives of the "Santa Claus Trust Fund Account Number 1225." All of the activities of the Christmas Secret Santa Sub-Account Number 1225.03 are categorized as nice. None the activities of the Christmas Secret Santa Sub-Account Number 1225.03 are categorized as naughty. That is the reason that the activities of the Christmas

Secret Santa Sub-Account Number 1225.03 will continue to operate as directed by the "Santa Claus Trust Fund Account Number 1225."

The Christmas Santa Letters Sub-Account Number 1225.04 will continue to operate as a nice Santa Claus Sub-Account to ensure that the Christmas Santa Letters does promote the directives of the "Santa Claus Trust Fund Account Number 1225." All of the activities of the Christmas Santa Letters Sub-Account Number 1225.04 are categorized as nice. None the activities of the Christmas Santa Letters Sub-Account Number 1225.04 are categorized as naughty. That is the reason that the activities of the Christmas Santa Letters Sub-Account Number 1225.04 will continue to operate as directed by the "Santa Claus Trust Fund Account Number 1225."

The Santa Claus Bell Ringers for the Salvation Army Sub-Account Number 1225.05 will continue to operate as a nice Santa Claus Sub-Account to ensure that the Santa Claus Bell Ringers for the Salvation Army does promote the directives of the "Santa Claus Trust Fund Account Number 1225." All of the activities of the Santa Claus Bell Ringers for the Salvation Army Sub-Account Number 1225.05 are categorized as nice. None the activities of the Santa Claus Bell Ringers for the Salvation Army Sub-Account Number 1225.05 are categorized as naughty. That is the reason that the activities of the Santa Claus Bell Ringers for the Salvation Army Sub-Account Number 1225.05 will continue to operate as directed by the "Santa Claus Trust Fund Account Number 1225."

The Christmas Eve Santa Claus Deliveries Sub-Account Number 1225.06 will continue to operate as a nice Santa Claus Sub-Account to ensure that the Christmas Eve Santa Claus Deliveries does promote the directives of the "Santa Claus Trust Fund Account Number 1225." All of the activities of the Christmas Eve Santa Claus Deliveries Sub-Account Number 1225.06 are categorized as nice. None the activities of the Christmas Eve Santa Claus Deliveries Sub-Account Number 1225.06 are categorized as naughty. That is the reason that the activities of the Christmas Eve Santa Claus Deliveries Sub-Account Number 1225.06 will continue to operate as directed by the "Santa Claus Trust Fund Account Number 1225."

The Christmas Meals Sub-Account Number 1225.07 will continue to operate as a nice Santa Claus Sub-Account to ensure that the Christmas Meals does promote the directives of the "Santa Claus Trust Fund Account Number 1225."   All of the activities of the Christmas Meals Sub-Account Number 1225.07 are categorized as nice. None the activities of the Christmas Meals Sub-Account Number 1225.07 are categorized as naughty. That is the reason that the activities of the Christmas Meals Sub-Account Number 1225.07 will continue to operate as directed by the "Santa Claus Trust Fund Account Number 1225."

The Christmas Decorations Sub-Account0 Number 1225.08 will continue to operate as a nice Santa Claus Sub-Account to ensure that the Christmas Decorations does promote the directives of the "Santa Claus Trust Fund Account Number 1225."   All of the activities of the Christmas Decorations Sub-Account0 Number 1225.08 are categorized as nice. None the activities of the Christmas Decorations Sub-Account0 Number 1225.08 are categorized as naughty. That is the reason that the activities of the Christmas Decorations Sub-Account0 Number 1225.08 will continue to operate as directed by the "Santa Claus Trust Fund Account Number 1225."

The Christmas Candy Canes Sub-Account Number 1225.09 will continue to operate as a nice Santa Claus Sub-Account to ensure that the Christmas Candy Canes does promote the directives of the "Santa Claus Trust Fund Account Number 1225."   All of the activities of the Christmas Candy Canes Sub-Account Number 1225.09 are categorized as nice. None the activities of the Christmas Candy Canes Sub-Account Number 1225.09 are categorized as naughty. That is the reason that the activities of the Christmas Candy Canes Sub-Account Number 1225.09 will continue to operate as directed by the "Santa Claus Trust Fund Account Number 1225."

The Christmas Gingerbread House Sub-Account Number 1225.10 will continue to operate as a nice Santa Claus Sub-Account to ensure that the Gingerbread House does promote the directives of the "Santa Claus Trust Fund Account Number 1225." All of the activities of the Christmas Gingerbread House Sub-Account Number 1225.10 are categorized as nice. None the activities of the Christmas Gingerbread House Sub-Account Number 1225.10 are categorized as naughty. That is the reason that the activities of the Christmas Gingerbread House Sub-Account Number 1225.10 will continue to operate as directed by the "Santa Claus Trust Fund Account Number 1225."

The Christmas Fruitcake Sub-Account Number 1225.11 will continue to operate as a nice Santa Claus Sub-Account to ensure that the Christmas Fruitcake does promote the directives of the "Santa Claus Trust Fund Account Number 1225." All of the activities of the Christmas Fruitcake Sub-Account Number 1225.11 are categorized as nice. None the activities of the Christmas Fruitcake Sub-Account Number 1225.11 are categorized as naughty. That is the reason that the activities of the Christmas Fruitcake Sub-Account Number 1225.11 will continue to operate as directed by the "Santa Claus Trust Fund Account Number 1225."

The Christmas Ice-Skating Sub-Account Number 1225.12 will continue to operate as a nice Santa Claus Sub-Account to ensure that the Christmas Ice-Skating does promote the directives of the "Santa Claus Trust Fund Account Number 1225." All of the activities of the Christmas Ice-Skating Sub-Account Number 1225.12 are categorized as nice. None the activities of the Christmas Ice-Skating Sub-Account Number 1225.12 are categorized as naughty. That is the reason that the activities of the Christmas Ice-Skating Sub-Account Number 1225.12 will continue to operate as directed by the "Santa Claus Trust Fund Account Number 1225."

The Christmas Parade with Santa Claus Sub-Account Number 1225.13 will continue to operate as a nice Santa Claus Sub-Account to ensure that the Christmas Parade with Santa Claus does promote the directives of the "Santa Claus Trust Fund Account Number 1225." All of the activities of the Christmas Parade with Santa Claus Sub-Account Number 1225.13 are categorized as nice. None the activities of the Christmas Parade with Santa Claus Sub-Account Number 1225.13 are categorized as naughty. That is the reason that the activities of the Christmas Parade with Santa Claus Sub-Account Number 1225.13 will continue to operate as directed by the "Santa Claus Trust Fund Account Number 1225."

The Christmas Presents Sub-Account Number 1225.14 will continue to operate as a nice Santa Claus Sub-Account to ensure that the Christmas Presents does promote the directives of the "Santa Claus Trust Fund Account Number 1225." All of the activities of the Christmas Presents Sub-Account Number 1225.14 are categorized as nice. None the activities of the Christmas Presents Sub-Account Number 1225.14 are categorized as naughty. That is the reason that the activities of the Christmas Presents Sub-Account Number 1225.14 will continue to operate as directed by the "Santa Claus Trust Fund Account Number 1225."

The Christmas Trees Sub-Account Number 1225.15 will continue to operate as a nice Santa Claus Sub-Account to ensure that the Christmas Trees does promote the directives of the "Santa Claus Trust Fund Account Number 1225." All of the activities of the Christmas Trees Sub-Account Number 1225.15 are categorized as nice. None the activities of the Christmas Trees Sub-Account Number 1225.15 are categorized as naughty. That is the reason that the activities of the Christmas Trees Sub-Account Number 1225.15 will continue to operate as directed by the "Santa Claus Trust Fund Account Number 1225."

The Christmas Parties Sub-Account Number 1225.16 will continue to operate as a nice Santa Claus Sub-Account to ensure that the Christmas Parties does promote the directives of the "Santa Claus Trust Fund Account Number 1225." All of the activities of the Christmas Parties Sub-Account Number 1225.16 are categorized as nice. None the activities of the Christmas Parties Sub-Account Number

1225.16 are categorized as naughty. That is the reason that the activities of the Christmas Parties Sub-Account Number 1225.16 will continue to operate as directed by the "Santa Claus Trust Fund Account Number 1225."

The Christmas Carolers Sub-Account Number 1225.17 will continue to operate as a nice Santa Claus Sub-Account to ensure that the Christmas Carolers does promote the directives of the "Santa Claus Trust Fund Account Number 1225."   All of the activities of the Christmas Carolers Sub-Account Number 1225.17 are categorized as nice. None the activities of the Christmas Carolers Sub-Account Number 1225.17 are categorized as naughty. That is the reason that the activities of the Christmas Carolers Sub-Account Number 1225.17 will continue to operate as directed by the "Santa Claus Trust Fund Account Number 1225."

The Christmas Church Bells Sub-Account Number 1225.18 will continue to operate as a nice Santa Claus Sub-Account to ensure that the Christmas Church Bells does promote the directives of the "Santa Claus Trust Fund Account Number 1225."   All of the activities of the Christmas Church Bells Sub-Account Number 1225.18 are categorized as nice. None the activities of the Christmas Church Bells Sub-Account Number 1225.18 are categorized as naughty. That is the reason that the activities of the Christmas Church Bells Sub-Account Number 1225.18 will continue to operate as directed by the "Santa Claus Trust Fund Account Number 1225."

The Christmas Mistletoe and the Magical Kiss Sub-Account Number 1225.19 will continue to operate as a nice Santa Claus Sub-Account to ensure that the Christmas Mistletoe and the Magical Kiss does promote the directives of the "Santa Claus Trust Fund Account Number 1225."   All of the activities of the Christmas Mistletoe and the Magical Kiss Sub-Account Number 1225.19 are categorized as nice. None the activities of the Christmas Mistletoe and the Magical Kiss Sub-Account Number 1225.19 are categorized as naughty. That is the reason that the activities of the Christmas Mistletoe and the Magical

Kiss Sub-Account Number 1225.19 will continue to operate as directed by the "Santa Claus Trust Fund Account Number 1225."

The Christmas Snowman Sub-Account Number 1225.20 will continue to operate as a nice Santa Claus Sub-Account to ensure that the Christmas Snowman does promote the directives of the "Santa Claus Trust Fund Account Number 1225." All of the activities of the Christmas Snowman Sub-Account Number 1225.20 are categorized as nice. None the activities of the Christmas Snowman Sub-Account Number 1225.20 are categorized as naughty. That is the reason that the activities of the Christmas Snowman Sub-Account Number 1225.20 will continue to operate as directed by the "Santa Claus Trust Fund Account Number 1225."

The Christmas Mall Santa Claus and the Picture with that Christmas Mall Santa Claus Sub-Account Number 1225.21 will continue to operate as a nice Santa Claus Sub-Account to ensure that the Christmas Mall Santa Claus and the Picture with that Christmas Mall Santa Claus does promote the directives of the "Santa Claus Trust Fund Account Number 1225." All of the activities of the Christmas Mall Santa Claus and the Picture with that Christmas Mall Santa Claus Sub-Account Number 1225.21 are categorized as nice. None the activities of the Christmas Mall Santa Claus and the Picture with that Christmas Mall Santa Claus Sub-Account Number 1225.21 are categorized as naughty. That is the reason that the activities of the Christmas Mall Santa Claus and the Picture with that Christmas Mall Santa Claus Sub-Account Number 1225.21 will continue to operate as directed by the "Santa Claus Trust Fund Account Number 1225."

The Christmas Miracles Sub-Account Number 1225.22 will continue to operate as a nice Santa Claus Sub-Account to ensure that the Christmas Miracles does promote the directives of the "Santa Claus Trust Fund Account Number 1225." All of the activities of the Christmas Miracles Sub-Account Number 1225.22 are categorized as nice. None the activities of the Christmas Miracles Sub-Account Number

1225.22 are categorized as naughty. That is the reason that the activities of the Christmas Miracles Sub-Account Number 1225.22 will continue to operate as directed by the "Santa Claus Trust Fund Account Number 1225."

Since this trial involving the "Santa Claus Trust Fund Account Number 1225" worked out so magically. I decided that I would go out on a limb of a Christmas tree and so I wrote Santa Claus a Christmas Santa Claus letter in which I asked that my family be safe and healthy and I asked Santa Claus to help me find my wife. I figured that this would at least make God and Santa Claus smile.

It is best to be nice even if you have to go out of your way. Being nice makes life so much better than being a stumbling block to someone's plans. I, Titus Uno, Certified Public Accountant, Forensic Certified Public Accountant, and Chartered Global Management Accountant, have had some people be stumbling blocks to me, but I, Titus Uno, Certified Public Accountant, Forensic Certified Public Accountant, and Chartered Global Management Accountant, am still going strong in the be nice category of life. Maybe those that have been my stumbling blocks will catch on and become nice people.

Merry Christmas, to all the readers of this book.

Made in the USA
Monee, IL
13 June 2021